FROM CHUMP TO CHAMP: HOW INDIVIDUALS GO FROM GOOD TO GREAT

FROM CHUMP TO CHAMP: HOW INDIVIDUALS GO FROM GOOD TO GREAT

David Benzel

Printed in the United States of America.

ISBN 10: 1480132950
ISBN: 9781480132955

Dedicated to

Cyndi,

Ever patient and loving;

Tarah and Tyler,

Shining stars full of light.

TABLE OF CONTENTS

Section Two

Be Something New – Make a Quantum Leap

Section Three

<u>Do</u> Something New: Make a Significant Difference

Section Four

Have Something New: Make the Six Crucial Turns
of Chump to Champ Leadership

OVERVIEW

Have you ever noticed that some organizations are healthier, more productive, and more successful than others? From Boy Scout troops to Fortune 500 companies, some organizations achieve superstar status and become the obvious choice for our loyalty. As a corporate coach I've worked with many organizations that desire to be recognized as such a company by making the leap from good to great. Since an organization could be defined as a place where two or more are gathered together, even families can be included here.

Moving from good to great is extremely challenging for any organization for one obvious reason: they consist of individuals who are also not yet great. The individuals that make up any organization (or family) can be stuck in apathy, complacency, mediocrity, or just plain confusion. So it follows that in order for an organization to move from good to great, the individuals within it must first move from chump to champ. It is a journey that starts on the individual level.

This book is about all the journeys you've been on, the journey you are currently taking, and the ones you haven't yet taken. While the title, *Chump to Champ*, sounds rather light-hearted, this is serious business. I'm not saying it can't be fun. In fact, it's one of the most amazing endeavors a human being can take. It can also be the most challenging and meaningful undertaking of your life. After all, what could possibly be more important than letting go of what you are to become more of what you were meant to be?

Look back over your life right now. Think about the person you were ten years ago...fifteen years ago...or longer. In what areas of your life have you changed, grown, and developed into something more than what you were? Look even closer. Did those changes happen by accident? Or, was there a master plan to take you from point A to point B? In some cases, you may have become something new out of your own inspiration. In other cases, perhaps it was out of desperation – change, or else! Either way, hopefully you have changed in a direction you're proud of.

When you look back at the old you...do you feel a little amazed... even a little embarrassed? Is there a little voice in your head that admits, "Wow, I can't believe I was like that back then!" That's the "chump" part of your story. The new you is the "champ" part!

The word "chump", as used in this book, is not a disrespectful term. Chump just refers to "my former self – the way I used to be." Never refer to yourself as "a chump" in the present tense, because at this moment you are as good as you've decided to be. But there is so much more inside you!

Recognize that there is a new kind of "champ" waiting to get out. As the new champ arrives and you become something new, a look back will reveal the old you—the chump, the former self. It will put a smile on your face! If you continue to develop—at some point in the future—today's champ will look like yesterday's chump.

I remember when I thought a nutritious meal included white bread, adding salt to everything, drinking soft drinks and eating French fries. What a chump! My wife introduced me to a whole new way of eating and cooking that included high fiber, lower sodium, less sugar, many more fruits and vegetables, and drinking lots of water. I feel like a champ! I became a healthier eater and a healthier person.

A friend of mine joined my cycling group and she loves to talk about her transformation from chump to champ. She recalls her first few rides with the group, only fourteen months earlier, when she struggled to keep up with us at twenty miles an hour for a thirty mile ride. Her legs ached, her back hurt, and she couldn't keep her heart rate down. Thirty miles at that speed probably felt like going to the moon and back. Six months later she had become one of the strongest riders in the group, capable of leading a pace line at twenty-five miles per hour and enduring a hundred mile ride. To make this transformation she had to change her ideas about how long to ride, how fast to ride, and what body position to use. As she adapted to new concepts, her body adapted as well. Now, she's a champ!

After fifteen years as a water ski coach, I realized that some of the concepts I embraced and preached in my early years were only partially correct at best. What a chump! As I spent time around other athletes and other coaches I came to see more sophisticated techniques and theories that changed my approach. My coaching evolved because I let go of some strongly held beliefs so I could take on some new ones. I became a champ.

For many people, letting go of old ways is scary. However, I'm convinced that the primary reason for this fear is the absence of a strategy for becoming something new. Without a good plan or road map for change, it's easy to assume the transition will be the equivalent of a month wandering in the wilderness – danger, suffering, with no relief in sight and a strong possibility of failure.

But what if you had a plan to follow? What if there was a road map? Not only could you conquer the challenge before you today, but the art of becoming something new and improved could be a constant, lifelong activity, repeated over and over. Any area of your life could open to a chump to champ transformation. Every relationship, every activity, and every career opportunity would contain a doorway to champ-like status. You would seldom be stuck and never have to settle for mediocrity. This book is designed to give you a road map for the future chump to champ journey you wish to take.

"We cannot become what we want to be by remaining what we are."
—Max DePree, author of Leadership is an Art

INTRODUCTION

You must become something new before you will ever do something new, and you must do something new before you will have something new. I wish it wasn't true. I wish there was a shortcut to having new results, improved outcomes, and huge amounts of credibility, but the truth is that it's a journey. It is risky to begin any journey without an understanding of life's principles and even riskier without a plan. A good road map, guide, and plan distinguishes chumps from champs and tilts the chances of success in your favor. Success begins with who you are, not what you do. This book provides you a road map for how to make the journey from chump to champ.

The book is divided into four sections. In the first section, I share my personal story and my chump to champ transformation. It's a heartwarming story of a pair of water skis and the boy who loved them.

Each of us has a story to tell and this is mine, leading up to and including the revelations I had about getting different results in life. It was an eye-opener for me, and it revealed truths about life and truths about me

– some of which were difficult to admit. But the truth sets us free and if you identify with my story and participate in what follows, you will have your own fabulous story to tell.

In the second section, you will be introduced to the four-step process that evolved from the lessons I learned while taking the "long route." Your transformation can take much less time by following these four steps for becoming something new. That "something" is up to you to decide, but the steps are universal and they have stood the test of time. If you are faithful in your work, and use the exercises included here or in the "Chump to Champ Workbook" (highly recommended!), you will immediately separate yourself from 90% of the competition.

Why? Because they are not willing to change the vehicle they're driving as they try to get from point A to point B! If you're reading this book, it means that you are willing to grow and change to become something of even greater value.

The third section of the book assumes you now have the kind of thinking that allows you to do things differently than ever before, and you've mastered the principles for transforming yourself in any direction necessary to actually behave in new ways. In this section, you'll find specific action strategies for making yourself more valuable to any organization – including your family – by what you do, and for developing the skills of others around you in ways that enhance relationships and productivity. This entire process builds your personal power and your credibility in an authentic and positive way. Your days of feeling inadequate and incompetent are over. People will want to know what's on your mind, and they will want to be around you because your energy and fresh perspective is magnetic.

The fourth and final section of the book focuses on the opportunities of your new level of credibility and how it can manifest itself in six crucial leadership opportunities. After all, your only reason for taking a journey like this is to have different results when it comes to the everyday challenges of working with fellow employees, your customers, and your family.

What most people want in the workplace is familiar to all of us – to be believed, to be honored, to have credibility, and to be appreciated. They want to be respected for their knowledge, opinions, skills and efforts. When you have more credibility with those above you and below you, numerous things improve in your life:

- You enjoy more mature conversations and healthier relationships
- Co-workers trust you and your judgment more readily
- Conflicts are resolved in more constructive ways
- Followers are more motivated from within
- Your coaching efforts are more effective
- You receive quicker buy-in for new initiatives and changes

The sum total of the six items above usually means more value to the organization, more personal fulfillment, and usually more money. Instead of being like the majority of people who either complain that the politics are slanted against them or that their efforts are never noticed, you can achieve these results by taking a proactive approach.

Why not take your game – and your life – to another level? Athletes do it. Musicians do it. Entertainers do it. There is absolutely no reason why you can't reinvent yourself to enjoy greater success, better relationships, and more personal satisfaction at work and home. It's time to go from chump to champ!

"Everything is on its way to somewhere."
—*John Travolta as George Malley in the movie Phenomenon.*

SECTION ONE

A PERSONAL JOURNEY

CHAPTER 1

THE LAND OF BLONDE
HAIR AND BLUE LIPS

Have you ever found something at which you wanted to excel, but couldn't quite hit the high notes? Is there an activity in your life where your passion is first class, but your performance is definitely sitting in coach? It could be any activity from a passive hobby to an aggressive sport, from a part-time job to a CEO position at work. Each of us wants to excel somewhere – to hit a homerun or sink the winning putt. So, what's holding you back from realizing that winning feeling? Have you wondered how some people, who don't appear to hold any special traits, cruise past mediocrity and don't stop until they hit outstanding? Perhaps you've wished for the secret or some kind of strategy that would take you more than an inch forward.

If you're interested in a personal journey with a purpose and a destination with a prize, this book is designed to give you the map. You'll find the four-step strategy described here to be simple, effective, and applicable to any area of your life – home, work, school, sports, community, and every relationship.

I'll start by sharing my own chump to champ journey and why it took so long. My hope is that you'll learn from my mistakes. I want to give you a shortcut that may literally save you years of trial and error, and save your sanity as well. There is only one thing more satisfying than working hard, and that's working smart, but only if you get the results you want! It's time to start your chump to champ journey.

A Passion Discovered

I figured out the most awful and most wonderful truth at about the same time in grade school – although it was more awful than wonderful. I discovered that we children at Hiawatha Elementary were not all created equal when it came to talent. I learned that while most of my buddies were catching on to the math assignment, I was still trying to find what page we were on. I learned that for some reason most teachers liked me, and so did most of the other kids, but my questions offered up during science class usually drew a moan, or worse, a laugh. I also learned that on the play field I was fast on my feet and difficult to catch in games requiring elusive running. The same was true when we got to the skating rink. My legs made me fast. And so there I was, faced with a reality no one had prepared me for. Academically I was not the best, though I was successful at making friends and clearly distinguished as an athlete. I excelled at running and skating, the latter being significant for the majority of the year since this was Minneapolis, Minnesota.

Throughout junior high and high school my grades ever so gradually improved to the point that by my senior year I was a solid A – B student. For some reason, my only athletic exploits came on the swim team where, once again, I was a late bloomer. My senior year was the only season when I emerged as one of the top two back-strokers on the team and finally earned my high school letter. Somehow everyone, including me, ignored the running and skating gifts! It was also in my senior year that I discovered my ability to be on stage, and had no fear about what the audience thought of me. I grabbed a key role in the senior class play and had a blast being "on stage".

During these years it occurred to me that there is nothing quite as enviable as being really good at something – to stand out and distinguish oneself. The awful reality of being mediocre in so many areas could be offset if you could just discover where you excelled and where your star shone brightest.

For some reason I plodded along accepting mediocrity in so many areas of my life without purposefully searching for a place to shine. I realize now that this approach was not uniquely mine, and in fact many people spend their entire lives doing exactly that!

My college years represented more of the same. I worked my GPA from a freshman year 2.0 to a senior year 3.5 – it took me four years to figure out how to be a good student in college. I played in the concert band, but of course, third or fourth chair trombone was my customary place. I acted in a few plays and generally found social sciences and speech class to be my bright spots. I still enjoyed having an audience, but didn't have anything significant to say!

If anyone had asked me at the end of my senior year of college, "What are you really, really good at?" I would have been stumped. But there were two other questions I think I could have answered: "What do you love to do?" and "What do you care about, besides your family?" I absolutely loved to water ski, even though our family did not own a boat and my opportunities were limited to bumming ski rides off a few friends during the short Minnesota summer. The thing I cared about was my college – Augsburg College in the heart of Minneapolis. I knew it was a caring place with caring people, and while I didn't know what I'd do with my degree, I believed I was a better person for having gone there. These two answers held powerful clues to my future in spite of the fact that I didn't understand it at the time.

My family owned a summer cottage on a lake south of the city. It was during the summer after graduating from college that I joined a water ski club and bought a boat, giving myself daily access to a slalom course and ski jump for the first time. I was twenty-one years old and had not only found my passion, but discovered that I had a knack for it. I accomplished in days, or less, basic skills that took other people weeks or months to learn. I became obsessed with the competitive aspect of water skiing, spending every available moment practicing or reading about the people and strategies of my sport. I competed in my first tournament that summer and knew I was destined to carve my reputation here. For the first time in my life I knew what it meant to love something so much that to "eat, sleep, and drink" it 24/7 was not only acceptable – it was the best way to feel truly fulfilled.

I had a personal vision of becoming a national water ski champion, and I was willing to pay the price. We skied into the fall until the water and air temperatures made it unbearable. The next spring we started skiing about a week after the ice went off the lake. We had hot-water bottles in the boat to warm our feet from the numbing cold. During that winter I attended seminary in Chicago and budgeted my entire lifestyle around a monetary goal so I could afford to drive to Florida for two weeks of ski school during spring break.

TheLandofBLondhairandBLueLips

The second part of my personal equation was fulfilled the next fall when I was hired as an admissions counselor at Augsburg, where I recruited and counseled high school students and their parents about the attributes and benefits of attending my alma mater. It was during this time that my gift of being comfortable in front of an audience exposed another gift I didn't know I had. It became apparent that while on stage I had a sensitivity for my audience and what they needed to hear. I discovered an ability to adjust my message "off the cuff" according to the situation. I could speak extemporaneously and found that aspect of public speaking to be a rush.

For the next seven years I toiled away at my craft – water skiing – while serving the college in my professional role. As I made a name for myself locally, it became evident that my skiing skills were very average on a national level. Starting at age twenty-one and enduring the short summers of Minnesota placed me at a huge disadvantage. We jokingly referred to summer in Minnesota as the two weeks in July when the ice fishing wasn't so good! The jumping event was particularly hard on me. There were few people in my area that truly understood this event. The goal was to hurl your body at high speeds toward what looked like a barn door sticking up out of the lake, catapult yourself through the air and try to land with the helmet up and the skis down. More often than not it was the other way around for me. I truly believe people came from miles around just to watch me crash. When I finished jumping in many tournaments, it looked like someone was holding a yard sale. Scattered on the shoreline was all my equipment while the safety boat was dumping my delirious body back at the dock. One crowning moment of a sobering nature occurred when I actually crashed through the side-curtain of the ski jump at the regional championships, breaking the jump and several ribs! Having a passion, and even some talent, doesn't mean you know what you're doing…and clearly I did not.

CHAPTER 2

GETTING WARMER, BUT NOT CLOSE ENOUGH

During this period I had become quite frustrated and even angry. Winners are people who have gold medals and tall trophies – we all know that. I looked around my house and I didn't have any gold medals or tall trophies. So, since winners have these things and I had none, I therefore reasoned: I am a loser! I found this so unacceptable that I literally wrote my own definition of a winner. I redefined winning to mean this:

> **"Winning is ending each day being just a little better than you were that morning."**

I decided that if I could end each day with some determination that I had improved even slightly in some aspect of my skiing, I was winning. And if I could string enough of those days in a row, I was a "winner!" This became my quest and totally changed the mental aspect of my approach. My goal was to be an ever-improving version of myself – daily! I redefined the game itself and little did I know that this transformation would lead to an even bigger discovery!

While my new frame of mind was a big benefit to my morale, it still did not solve one of my challenges – I was in the wrong place. In spite of my determination, self-discipline, and natural athletic gifts, lacking the correct information, techniques and strategies just meant I was getting more consistent at doing things incorrectly! If your dream is to become a national water ski champion and you live in Minnesota, there comes a time when you need to come to grips with reality! I felt like the water ski-ing equivalent of the Jamaican Bobsled Team – what am I doing here? I realized the need for change. Not a little adjustment, but a revolutionary change – a radical change. One that would take courage to make, but would have dramatic and transformational results.

Before going on, it's important to introduce my partner, who was so influential in the next big decision. After competing for four seasons, I qualified for the national championships and met my wife-tobe at that event. She had been competing since age eleven and had already been a girl's division national champion. Through pure finesse and some very suave maneuvers, I tricked this California beauty into marrying me and moving to Minnesota! Am I good or what? However, after a year and a half of marriage and two very long and cold winters, Cyndi opened my eyes to some new possibilities.

At the age of twenty-nine and a half, I rented out our house (only to sell it later), sold one car, and both of us quit our jobs! Cyndi was a dental hygienist and I had become Director of Admissions at Augsburg by this time. I had been competing for eight seasons and I recognized the need to associate with skiers, coaches, and a climate that would take me to the next level. It was time to make a major change, as risky as it seemed. Most of our friends thought we were crazy. We were giving up our careers, our income, our home, as well as leaving our friends, my family, and everything I'd ever known…to do what? To go chase buoys and crash off ski jumps in warmer weather? And yet some of our friends would admit that while it was risky to chase one's dream, they wished they had the courage to do the same.

We spent the next six years skiing full-time and coaching to finance this lifestyle. We spent approximately six months of each year coaching and training at a ski school on the high desert of southern California where we lived in an eight by thirteen foot travel trailer for the first three summers. It was so small you had to step outside to change your mind! We spent the other six months (winters) in Florida working at another ski school. We drove back and forth across the country twice each year with all our earthly possessions, chasing our dreams.

I wish I could report that upon leaving Minnesota and putting myself in a warmer climate year round, my performance issues disappeared and my vision was realized. Not hardly! Location is an important factor, and even more so is the exposure to people who know more than you. But, you still must do the work, learn the skills, overcome the bad habits, and most importantly...win the mental game. No, it wasn't a slam-dunk for me at all. I struggled for four more years after leaving Minnesota before I finally won a national title. But, then I won six consecutive national overall titles, plus two event titles, and broke my division's national jump record five times. That's a lot more fun than crashing through the side-curtain of a ski jump!

CHAPTER 3

THE PERFORMANCE EQUATION

At this point I hope you're wondering what transpired that took me from crash expert to medal winner – from chump to champ – in the blink of twelve years! This is where the lesson really begins. For the longest time, I focused on the physical skills and skiing strategies that I saw in great skiers. I put 100% of my effort into conditioning, time on the water, and eating right. I figured that if practicing three times a day is good, then six times a day is better! And if four days a week is good, then five or six days a week is what I'll do. No doubt I needed a lot of practice, but I was missing an important strategy that great performers in every sport and in every arena know. It's not about bending your knees and keeping your eyes on the trees! It's not about the flex in your skis or the strength of the breeze! Or, as Lance Armstrong wrote, "It's not about the bike." My missing element hit me square in my helmet when I realized that I practiced like a champ and competed like a chump! In other words, what I could do Monday through Friday in practice is not what I delivered on the weekends in tournaments when it counted. And the guys on the dock just laugh when you tell them how well you're skiing in practice! Who cares!

I had a great vision for myself. I had set worthy and lofty goals. I was in the best physical condition of my life. And besides that, I had the best equipment money could buy.

Then it occurred to me. Wham! I've got a thousand dollars worth of high tech carbon graphite skis on my feet and a five-cent mental approach in my helmet!

I was trying to win a game with only muscle, when the secrets to success were hiding between my ears. I realized the last two elements of the strategy were missing – what I now believe to be the most important parts. When I learned how to win the mental battle and how to overcome the obstacles of my own mind, I made my move from chump to champ. Not just a little improvement, but a giant gain. As if a rubber band had been stretched and stretched, pulled tight and ready to unleash stored energy, and I had finally found the trigger to release my potential and turn it into performance when it mattered. Everything I needed was inside me, but I had to learn how to get myself out of the way and let it happen. Once I learned this strategy, my tournament performances were equal to or better than what I did in practice. My consistency became a point of confidence for me and a force in the mind of my competitors. But like many others, I had been held back for years by failing to understand the chump to champ strategy in its entirety. And, to be honest, it's easy to understand how this happens and continues to happen to people in any endeavor.

We can use a simple math equation to demonstrate why some performances are successful and why some are not.

$$
\begin{array}{ccc}
\text{TALENTS} & & \text{TALENTS} \\
+ \text{STRATEGY} & \text{OR} & + \text{STRATEGY} \\
\underline{\pm \text{EFFORT}} & & \underline{\pm \text{EFFORT}} \\
= \text{Success} & & = \text{Lesson}
\end{array}
$$

Each of us has been given certain talents. We were hardwired with a set of talents that are unique to us. We were not given a full deck of talents, just a unique combination of the talents from the master list of talents. Then we each go out into the world and attempt to perform using whatever strategies we think will work. That's one of the reasons people do things differently; why some kids swing a bat differently than others; why some salespeople talk more than others; why some coaches use discipline more than others – they think it works. The last variable is how much effort we choose to expend – how much time we put in, how many practices we go to, how much energy we invest. Regardless of the specifics, when all three variables are added up, there are varying degrees of success achieved. Some would say there is success and there is failure. I've always believed there is no such thing as failure – there are only lessons, which is the same as delayed success. We are delayed from our success until the lessons are learned. We can't experience true success until we learn each lesson, but we have not failed, unless we quit and refuse to continue learning.

What we all wonder when we are faced with something other than success, is why are we not experiencing success? What's not working? In some cases the reason is hidden in the amount, or lack, of effort. We often seek the path of least resistance, which is called comfort, and refuse to get uncomfortable. New performance levels usually require some discomfort because there is a change that must take place in us. We must give up some old part of ourselves to take on a new part, and that takes effort and discomfort.

However, I have come to believe that when faced with repeated poor performances, or delayed successes, a vast number of us begin to question our talents and ourselves. We slip into self-doubt very easily and begin to wonder if perhaps we just don't have what it takes to get this done right. We know others are more talented than us and it begins to haunt us that the problem is really inside! "Oh my, maybe I can't do it!" Or, perhaps, your private nightmare is, "I am inadequate," although these thoughts are seldom spoken out loud. I'll admit to having days when I feared that I didn't have the right stuff – that I'd never really "get it." Only my stubborn determination kept me going.

Here's the good news: For 99% of what you want to do in your life, you have everything you need, except perhaps the right strategy. There's nothing wrong with you! I didn't say you can do everything. I said you can do the things you truly want to do — the things you have a natural passion for — and do them in an outstanding way!

You do not have to settle for mediocrity. The part of the equation that deserves your full attention is STRATEGY!

If you're not getting the results you want, you are not using the right STRATEGY! You may have tried many things, but not the right one yet, so keep trying!

Where in your life do you have a desire to be transformed? Where is it that you'd like to make a significant change? Is it in a relationship, a business, a sport, a hobby, or in your own self-esteem? If you are willing to change, your world will change with you.

The Performance equaTion

The next section of this book is about the four-step strategy I discovered and implemented in my life. But there's more. After discovering how it transformed my skiing career, I started asking successful athletes in other sports about my theory for quantum leap performances. I wanted to know if other peak performers were purposefully taking advantage of the powerful relationship between their dreams, selected targets, a vivid imagination, and a positive belief system. Next I asked successful entrepreneurs and business leaders. Then I asked people who had successful relationships with spouses and family members. What I learned was that almost all of them used some version of my strategy, even if they didn't realize it! It is a universal strategy for achieving personal excellence in any area of life, regardless of the endeavor, your age, or number of years you've struggled. A chump to champ transformation – a quantum leap – is possible for anyone in any situation if they choose to use the four steps of the formula. The sad thing is that so many people don't know the strategy, they don't have a plan, or they've wasted years trying things that don't get it done. Hoping for new results is not a strategy. A method that works is required.

SECTION TWO

BE SOMETHING NEW – MAKE A QUANTUM LEAP

To truly be something new takes some effort. This effort should be purposeful. It needs a design and a desired outcome that is clear. I chose to be a national water ski champion in my mind long before the gold medal arrived. What do you choose to be? In this section you'll find a description of the four steps, plus a "how to" section for making your quantum leap. The "Chump to Champ Workbook" will provide you with more detailed exercises and assistance in following the four steps.

CHAPTER 4

STEP 1 – DREAM

Declare Your Destination

The year was 1988, and the big shoot-out in the Women's Long Figure Skating Program at the Winter Olympics was between Debbie Thomas of the U.S. and Katerina Witt of East Germany. When the judges finished their evaluations Katerina Witt was crowned the gold medalist. As her national anthem was played and she ascended the steps to the first place riser to receive her gold medal, another dramatic ceremony was taking place miles and miles away in Sewell, New Jersey. A young five-year old girl by the name of Tara Lipinski was walking to the top of makeshift risers in her living room; her father placed a homemade gold medal around her neck, as she pretended to be Katerina Witt. Exactly ten years later, at age fifteen, Tara Lipinski became the youngest gold medalist when she won the 1998 Olympics Figure Skating event – for real! When did her dream begin? As we now know, it began ten years earlier in her living room. What a great example of the power of a dream!

The question is: What's *your* dream? Let's first make sure you understand what it is and why it's so powerful. A dream is simply a picture in your head of what you'd like to be, like to do, or like to have at some point in the future. It comes from your imagination and the desires of your heart. As far as we know, human beings are the only animals in the kingdom that have this gift of imagination. When we use this gift, we're able to give ourselves a vivid picture of how we'd like things to be. Just think of the amazing things in our world that began with someone's vivid imagination of what "could be" instead of "what was." Thomas Edison imagined the light bulb before it was his invention. Henry Ford imagined a car for every family before the Model T went into production. And Walt Disney imagined Epcot long before its reality. Nothing that you see around you came into existence without it first being a desire and a dream in someone's head.

Your dream answers the question: "Where am I going?" Surprisingly, most people don't have a clear dream, and it's usually because of one reason: They haven't decided what it is they want to be, want to do, or want to have! They're so busy working with their head down, that they haven't taken the time to pull their head up and look out at the horizon and choose a point toward which to march.

Take a moment now to shift your attention to *your* dream. Grab a piece of paper and write: "MY _____ DREAM" across the top. Then decide what area of your life you're dreaming about. Is it your family life, your financial life, your career or work life, or perhaps your spiritual life? Perhaps you are involved in a sport or hobby to which you've committed a lot of time and energy, and you find yourself wishing for a higher level of performance or a different kind of experience. That's dreaming! It could even be in regard to a specific relationship in your life where you want something more for the future. If you're serving a role in your church or your community and the desires of your heart have you yearning for some outcome, you are dreaming something! You can have a dream for each of these areas, but for now pick one and fill in the blank.

Dreaming is a natural human experience, but many people don't understand what they're doing or the potential power of it. Some will call it daydreaming and just dismiss it. Big mistake! Daydreaming is a way in which we learn the desires of our heart. Great artists and musicians know how to capture those daydreams and turn them into a painted canvas or a sheet of music. They recognize the daydream as a vision of something they want.

Why is it important to know what you want? I heard a story from my sport psychologist friend, Dr. Rob Gilbert, about a schoolteacher who divided her third grade class into three groups. Each group was given a jigsaw puzzle box full of pieces and the students were instructed to put the puzzle together without talking to each other. The first group received a box with a pretty mountain scene on the cover. The second group received a box with a blank cover – no picture at all. The third group had a picture on the cover of a serene river running through a valley – however, this group's pieces did not match the cover of the box...a detail of which they were completely unaware! As you can imagine the outcome of each group was significantly different.

The first group, in spite of the "no talking" rule, assembled their puzzle because everyone had a clear picture of what the end product should look like. They had a common vision. The second group struggled and actually got bored with the assignment very quickly because they lacked any kind of vision. The third group had a vision, but it was the wrong vision for the pieces in the box. They were pursuing a vision for which they were not equipped. They didn't have a strategy that would work.

Select an area of your life where you know the desires of your heart, and write down a dream of what you see for yourself in the future. Don't limit yourself by your current circumstances. When I dreamed of being a national water ski champion for the very first time, I was still living in Minnesota and driving my car across a frozen lake to go ice fishing! Dream big! If you don't yet have a dream, just keep reading and use the "How to Identify Your Dream" helpers at the end of this chapter.

"If your heart is in your dream, no request is too extreme." — Jiminy Cricket

So, what should you do with this dream now that you have one? Let's assume you wrote a dream related to your family-life like this: "I have a dream of our family moving to the country where we can have more space for our children, where we have big trees for shade and a bigger house with more living space." If you were the author of this dream and you really wanted these things, you'd be extremely motivated every time you thought about it! So, what's the first thing you'd do? You would run into the kitchen, call the entire family together and almost shout, "I have a dream!" And then you would share your dream with great enthusiasm. Your passion would fill the room. You would describe all the details as best as you could see them right now. And if it were a really big dream, far away from the present reality, most of the people in the room would look at you like you're crazy! They would call it "wishful thinking." They might tell you that you've been dreaming, which is exactly the truth! Don't you think people looked at Edison, Ford, and Disney exactly that way? They thought these guys were a little crazy…until they learned that these men knew how to turn dreams into reality!

The most important ingredient is the energy behind the dream. Ask yourself, "Is my desire genuine? Is my dream clear? And does it get me excited about the future?" I didn't really care if my friends approved of my dream. I knew what I wanted. If you know what you want, the energy that comes from within is far more important than the approval coming from without. The energy that surrounds your dream is an intangible secret weapon that has the potential to overcome all naysayers and all obstacles. Hence the expression, "If the dream is big enough the facts don't count." Don't let anyone steal your dream.

When I traveled to London as coach of the U.S. Water Ski Team for the 1987 World Championships, we encountered several circumstances that seemed unfavorable to our chances of realizing our dream, which was to win another team world title. At that time, the U.S. Water Ski Team had the longest standing string of team world titles of any U.S. athletic team. We were undefeated in every world championship since the beginning of such team events in 1949. However, the pressure was building, and teams from France, England, Australia, and Canada were closing in on us. For the first time, team members began noticing and commenting on some of the potentially negative circumstances we faced. First of all, there was some complaining about the water being much colder than what we were accustomed to back in Florida. Secondly, someone pointed out how different the food was and how much their eating habits were being compromised by this change. Perhaps the most significant factor was the fact that we'd be skiing behind a boat manufactured in Europe, which was never used in our tournaments in the U.S. Therefore, the wake was larger, shaped differently, and felt very unfamiliar. Each factor carried varying significance for each athlete, and everyone was aware of these distractions.

Two skiers on the team had a different response to these factors, and this response came from their own personal convictions about why they had come to London. Their personal dreams about winning, and the energy behind those dreams, generated a confidence that was more powerful than water temperature, food, or boat wakes. In fact every time they heard a negative comment about anything, they would mumble just loud enough for a few people to hear, "It just doesn't matter." This subtle campaign began to spread through the group as an ideal way to dismiss anything that might rob us of our focus or our determination. It served notice that there would be no excuses. It just didn't matter what obstacles we encountered. We were there for a reason and nothing (not cold water, weird food, or strange boats) would deter us from realizing our dream! As it turned out, we kept the string of victories alive.

Great dreams are always accompanied by high levels of positive energy, fueled by desire and hope, never to be denied.

How TO Identify Your Dream

I. Here are some questions to stimulate your thinking about your dreams of the future. If you could look past the horizon, what would you see?

1. If you could live anywhere, where would you live?
2. If you could have any career, what work would you do?
3. If you could advance in any sport, game, or hobby, which one would you choose and what performance would you have?
4. If you could make one significant change in yourself physically, what would it be?
5. If you could make one significant change in yourself emotionally, what would it be?
6. If you could make one significant change in yourself intellectually, what would it be?
7. If you could make one significant change in yourself spiritually, what would it be?

8. If you could make one significant change in your work habits, what would it be?

9. If you could make one significant change in your organizational skills, what would it be?

10. If you could make one significant change in your communication skills, what would it be?

11. If you could make one significant improvement in your home life what would it be?

12. If you could make one significant improvement in your lifestyle, what would it be?

13. If you could make one significant improvement in your community or civic organization, what would it be?

14. If you could make one significant change in your social life or love life, what would it be?

II. From your answers above, choose the three or four that trigger an emotional response – positive or negative. Which answers excite you and the thought of the change invigorates you? Which answers create some anxiety because the change scares you even though it's something you want? For the moment, focus on the answers that contain the most energy for you, and write them below.

1.

2.

3.

4.

III. From your list of the top three or four, choose the one that would come the closest to keeping you awake at night if you absolutely knew it was going to happen.

1.

CHAPTER 5

STEP 2 – AIM

Identify Your Targets and Take Aim

In the absence of a worthwhile target, people tend to focus on what they don't want to happen. A racecar driver racing through the highly banked turns at the Daytona Speedway must focus on what he wants, which is to come down off the turn in control and in position. For this reason he focuses his eyes forward and left through the turn. What he does not want is to hit the wall, but all drivers will tell you that if you allow your eyes to gaze at the wall, you're going there!

Leroy flew the parasail for the Prior Lake Ski Show in Minnesota in the mid-seventies. After reaching maximum elevation using his 500' tow rope, Leroy pulled the release to make his ceremonial descent into the lake at the beginning of our ski show. On one occasion however, Leroy looked down and found himself starring at the ski jump anchored in the middle of the lake. An unusual thought entered his mind. "I certainly hope I don't land on the ski jump." Throughout his descent he became increasingly concerned with this one negative outcome. The ski jump was exactly 14 feet by 22 feet while the lake was approximately 100 acres in size. In spite of these disproportionate dimensions – you guessed it – Leroy landed on the jump and broke his leg. In the absence of a positive goal, people tend to focus on avoiding a negative outcome which only increases the chances of getting exactly that!

However most people are not very fond of goals. I suppose that's why so few actually set goals, not to mention write them down. I heard a guy ask a friend of mine, "What's your goal?" My friend responded, "Don't have one." "Well, you'll certainly hit that!" came the reply.

There are a number of reasons for this. Many people don't know what they want. How can you set a goal if you haven't decided what you're trying to achieve? Others know what they want but don't know how to create a worthwhile goal that actually works for them. And then there are those who fear the pressure of a goal, and don't want to face themselves – or others – when they miss the mark or give up on a goal.

The people who are most committed to the process of setting and achieving goals are the ones who have had successful experiences with them. They are true believers and faithful disciples of goal setting because they have reaped the benefits of this magical process. Yes, magical – but we'll get to that in a moment. First, let's figure out where people learn about using goals as a way of getting more of what they want.

It appears that most of us didn't learn about goal setting in a formal classroom setting. We witnessed our parents talking about goals at work, or an older sibling referring to a team goal or a personal goal of making a team. In fact, most people who refer to a goal, use it incorrectly, and are actually referring to a dream – not a goal at all. A dream and a goal are not the same, although they are closely related.

We've discussed that a dream is a picture in our head of how life should be if we could wave a magic wand and change it. We are referring to what we want to be, do, or have. On the other hand, a goal is a specific target that must be hit, or an activity that must be repeated, that makes it possible for the dream to become a reality. Dreams that are not backed up with specific goals will often remain just unrealized visions.

A really good goal refers to some action that, if done well enough or often enough, will result in the dream turning from fantasy to fact. It is the workhorse of accomplishment and the action verb of dreams. When you find yourself knowing what it is you want in life, you've answered the question "What?" When you know what targets must be hit (goals), you've answered the question "How?" When someone says they want a house on the ocean, that's not really a goal – it's a dream. A goal would sound like this: "I will save $500.00 each month for a down payment on my new ocean-front home." Or, "I will spend four days each month going to open house events in search of an ocean home I can afford." These targets are the individual steps that must be climbed.

Properly stated goals are very specific and very measurable. On any given day you can check your progress to see if you are closer to hitting your goal, stuck in the same place, or farther away! That's why setting a goal to lose ten pounds by June 1st works, and saying "I've set a goal to be thinner" doesn't work. Without a deadline or a method of measuring, there's actually no such thing as a progress report.

If you watch the movie, *Miracle*, starring Kurt Russell as Coach Herb Brooks of the 1980 U.S. Olympic Hockey team, you'll find an interesting discussion about aspirations for the team. In the opening scenes of the movie, Brooks tells the officials of USA Hockey that his goal is to beat the Soviets at the 1980 Olympics. I believe that sounds more like a true dream. His dream was to be Olympic champions; his goal was to teach the U.S. Team a new style of hockey – a hybrid of the Canadian style and the Soviet style. Another goal was to improve the conditioning of the American skaters so they could skate with the Soviets for three periods of hockey without running out of gas! A third goal was to play a tougher and longer season. Goals are most useful when progress can be measured, and when reaching multiple goals turns a dream into a reality. As we know, the 1980 U.S. Hockey Team did exactly what they set out to do.

In another example, President Kennedy rallied a nation in his famous "going to the moon" speech in May of 1961. He said that "it should be our mission" by the end of the decade to put a man on the moon and bring him back safely. It could be argued that he was stating a very big goal – a specific, measurable, action oriented, realistic, and time-based goal. His dream was for America to lead the world in space exploration. At that moment, the Soviets had the edge by launching the first satellite to orbit the earth in October of 1957. The challenge of his goal inspired an energetic response from the American people and the scientific community.

Americans believed in the goal. They did not wonder *if* we'd get to the moon; they wondered *when* we'd get to the moon.

Athletes concerned with wins and businesses concerned with sales are the biggest proponents of goal setting. Through experience, they have learned what I call the magic of a goal. Something mysterious happens once a goal is set, and especially once it's written down. When you write a goal on a piece of paper and sign your name, it takes on heightened significance. Its importance is amplified in your mind, and your subconscious is now aware and engaged in the process. The act of writing the goal down and reading it out loud gives it special psychological status. Consequently, your brain and your eyes begin to work together in a new way. They collaborate in recognizing any and all information or stimuli that is in any way related to the goal. You will begin to notice opportunities, resources, and ideas that were invisible to you before, but are now evident and useful to you.

Have you ever wanted a particular new car? Have you noticed that once you made it a goal to own that particular car you started seeing more of them? You also discovered new places to buy and alternative ways to finance your goal. Have you noticed that when it's extremely important to you to take a long expensive trip, you begin stumbling upon the many ways to travel economically on planes, trains, and automobiles? Those creative options were not obvious to you before, but they were always there. The declaration of a goal puts our senses into overdrive seeking out ways to hit the goal. It's as if the universe cooperates to bring you closer to goal achievement. Conversely, if there is no goal, there's no need for the magic! Your senses remain neutral and all the valuable resources you need blend into the scenery.

Focus

There's one other healthy side effect of an established goal – most people refer to it as laser-like focus. If you've ever tried to thread a sewing needle you understand the nature of a narrow focus. While attempting to thread a needle, everything else in your field of vision goes blurry – or out of focus. This is necessary in order for you to run that tiny bit of thread through the tiny opening of a needle. By definition, to truly focus on something means that other things must be slightly out of focus. If everything is equally focused, then nothing is particularly focused. In other words, everything is of equal importance.

Nothing extraordinary can be accomplished in that manner. When a baseball pitcher decides to skim the inside corner of the plate with his fastball, he is narrowly focused on that part of the plate – while trying not to be distracted by the runner talking a large lead off first base. If too distracted by the runner, the fastball is more likely to miss its mark. Focus, therefore, has to do with the amount of attention we give something, and there's only so much to go around. Experts say most of us can truly focus on only two major goals in our lives at one time because of the attention required to accomplish important goals. You will notice, when we are really passionate about a goal, our focus sharpens, our energy and determination are heightened, and we are capable of amazing things. Watch a wide receiver catch a football while being covered by three defenders. Watch a golfer sink a fifteen-foot putt with thousands of fans watching and millions of dollars on the line. Watch a pianist performing an intricate piece of music with both hands and feet working the piano simultaneously, yet flawlessly.

Focus is something we can bring to a moment, or to a month long or yearlong project. Watch the mother of four children focus on her tone of voice each day because she's committed to sending calm messages to her children, despite the circumstances. Watch the father, who's working two jobs to make ends meet, focus on a math problem with his son because it's his goal to be involved with his son's education. Focus is a by-product of a clearly defined goal…and it works like magic!

Obstacles

Before you even begin to move toward your targets, know that you will encounter obstacles and you will need to overcome those obstacles. Of course there are obstacles! If there were no obstacles you would already have what you want. Those obstacles are the reason you are not where you want to be, or are not the person you hope to become. And when you identify those obstacles, just remember, "Momma said there'd be days like this."

Obstacles can be bad habits, like a batter who doesn't keep his eye on the ball. They can be resources like not enough money to buy needed equipment. Obstacles can be a lack of knowledge or information, which must be obtained. Or it could even be location, like living in Minnesota when your passion is water skiing – lots of lakes, but lousy weather too many months of the year!

Obstacles are different for everyone, and they are overcome in different ways. I've found that when the dream is big enough and the passion strong enough, people are incredibly resourceful in removing obstacles. They just figure out a way! On the other hand, if the dream is not a powerful dream, but instead a "wish" then almost any excuse will do for allowing an obstacle to stop all progress.

We owned a home in Minnesota when we began contemplating our big radical change in lifestyle. I could have said, "We can't go to warmer weather because we have this house!" "What on earth will we do with the house?" We also had good jobs. "I can't leave my career because I'm just beginning to move up the ladder in this organization." "And besides, what will people think of me." We had lots of friends in Minnesota and had no friends where we were going, except for one family in Newberry Springs, CA. I could have said, "I can't give up all my friends." "I don't know anyone there." When people are not committed to their dream, any excuse will do! "I can't pursue my dreams now, - my favorite TV show is coming on."

Attack all obstacles knowing there's a solution just waiting to be found. Never surrender!

How TO <u>Aim</u> For Your Targets

I. With your number one dream clearly in mind, think of an activity that must be done to reach that dream. Write down an activity that would erase an obstacle, or provide a skill, or provide a resource that you need. This activity must be measurable in some way in order to qualify as a target and not just another dream.

Example:

Dream: Become a faster runner.

Improper target: Move my legs faster (This is just another way of expressing the dream).

Improper target: Improve my technique (This is not sufficient to qualify as a target).

A proper target you can aim for: "Add one high intensity interval workout to each week's training schedule where I maintain a time of _____ seconds for each of six sprints"

Example:

Dream: Have a closer and more satisfying relationship with my wife.

Improper target: "Improve my communication skills." (Since we can't measure the word "improve" this is more of a dream than a target.)

A proper target you can aim for: "Set aside one night every week as date night for my wife and I to enjoy an evening of private conversation."

Example:

> **Dream:** Become the top sales representative in my department.
>
> **Improper target:** Outwork all other sales reps. (How will you measure "outwork"?)
>
> **A proper target you can aim for:** Make 20% more outgoing phone calls each week to prospective clients than the office average from the week before.
>
> **A proper target you can aim for:** Increase my referrals by 15% by spending one evening a week making follow-up contacts to former clients.

Write your number one target here._____

_____

_____

II. Write additional targets that come to mind which are measurable and will assist you in reaching your Dream.

_____

_____

_____

III. Transfer your targets to a special piece of paper (special size or unique color) and find a place to display your targets where you will see them regularly. This can be a wall in your office, next to the mirror in your bathroom, or on the refrigerator in the kitchen. Read your goals (out loud if possible) at least once per day.

IV. Share your intentions to hit these targets with at least one other person with whom you share a special relationship.

V. Create a simple scorecard upon which you can keep track of the quantity and quality of your activity. It's very important to check and record progress. This feedback lets you know if your activity is having the effect you desire. A bathroom scale provides feedback for someone trying to lose weight and lets him or her know whether his or her diet activities are working. You can depend on this simple truth: what gets measured, gets improved.

CHAPTER 6

STEP 3 – IMAGINE

Play Your Movie In Your Mind

Traditional three-event water skiing has three disciplines: slalom (rounding six buoys per pass using a rope that is shortened after each pass), trick skiing (think figure skating on a small water ski), and jumping (longest jump wins). Most skiers who choose to compete in all three will inevitably find themselves weaker in one of the three events. For our daughter Tarah, it was jumping. She liked the other two events more, practiced them more, and had some fear of jumping, which is normal and healthy. One day in April of her junior year of high school, she came to me after a frustrating jump ride and said she was thinking about quitting jumping. "I'm not making any progress and it doesn't come naturally for me" she said. I was certain she understood that by removing herself from the jump event she automatically gave up being considered for an overall title (similar to the "All-Around" in gymnastics) at any tournament she entered and believed the issue had more to do with whether or not she "saw herself" as a jumper. So, this is what I told her.

"The story of Tarah's jumping career can be told in one of two ways. One way is that Tarah was originally a three-event skier whose jumping wasn't very strong. She got discouraged during her high school years and decided to give it up and has been a slalom and trick skier ever since. Or, the story could be told that Tarah was a three-event skier who struggled with jumping and for a long time wasn't very strong in that event. However, she was determined to raise her jumping to a new level. During her high school years, Tarah refocused her efforts and began studying video of excellent women jumpers. She increased her training time in jumping, solicited the coaching of some of the world's best jumpers and spent time with them. She increased her strength and confidence with her extra work and now she doesn't have a weak event anymore."

I told Tarah that either of these two scenarios was alright with me. She could choose either storyline for her movie, which would play in the theater of her mind. She would be the star and producer of her movie. She could direct the movie, sell the tickets and popcorn, as well as run the projector. She could determine how the story would end because she is the writer of this story! It's her movie.

In August of that same season, Tarah won a national jump title in her age division at the U.S. National Championships. She found a love for jumping and became a very accomplished jumper by deciding how she wanted her movie to play, and then playing it in the theater of her mind.

The best language you can use when talking to your brain is pictures. Our brains think in pictures. Even the words we choose create pictures. When we imagine ourselves being cool and confident under pressure, those kinds of pictures are created and recorded by our subconscious. If our subconscious receives those pictures often enough, our behavior will be modified to fit the pictures. If we imagine ourselves as angry and out of control under pressure, the opposite types of pictures are created and recorded by our subconscious. Behaviors that fit those pictures will begin to manifest themselves in our life. The subconscious brain is eager for information about what we want, but it does not judge the information we send it as good or bad, right or wrong. It just accepts it, and assumes we want it. Consequently, when we imagine things we don't want, our subconscious brain is still assuming we want it!

I watched a young member of our water ski training center staff jumping in one of our tournaments. He took a terrible crash that left his equipment scattered over three zip codes! It was horrendous. As they carried him from the water he looked up at me and said, "I was lying in bed last night worried that this might happened today." I thought to myself, "Well, you got what you asked for." Yes, he asked for it! While lying in bed hoping that he wouldn't crash in the tournament, pictures of a crash are automatically being created and recorded by his subconscious brain. The word "crash" creates a picture. The brain collects that picture and thinks, "Looks to me like my little friend here wants to come off the jump tomorrow with both tips down, trailing his out-of-control flailing body all the way to the water

– I can arrange that – no problem!" The more vivid and frequent the images created, the more likely they will be manifested in real life.

You may be thinking, "But he was thinking that he didn't want to crash." True, but there is no picture for negative words like don't, won't, no, can't, or not. So the phrase "Don't crash" actually equals "Crash" and will produce the appropriate picture to go along with it. The only way to avoid a crash is to spend your time thinking about and talking about beautiful, under-control, excellent jumps, which will produce the most desirable pictures for your subconscious brain to manifest. We must spend time imprinting our subconscious with what we want – instead of what we don't want.

Much writing and research has been dedicated to the effects of positive imagery on athletic performance. The East German Olympic program taught the visualization techniques to their athletes in the 60s and 70s. Great golfers and platform divers learned to imagine their next performance a week in advance of the next competition. POWs reported their experiences of mentally rehearsing a round of golf each day in prison, and coming home to shoot par! The truth is that the concept of using our senses (sight, hearing, smelling, touch, and taste) in the theater of our mind is an ancient lesson found in many writings before the time of Christ. "As a man thinks in his heart, so he is," comes from the book of Proverbs (23:7) in the Bible and was written in the eighth century BC. The concept is not new. It's well established that mental rehearsal works to increase the probability of a desired outcome. We become whatever it is we think about most. Scientists tell us that the same neurological pathways are triggered in a vividly imagined scenario as are triggered in the real performance.

The greater mystery is why people don't purposefully use this technique more often to improve their performance in every area of their life.

For instance, if you would like to speak in front of large audiences with complete composure and confidence, why not rehearse that scene in your mind over and over exactly the way you want it to go? The subconscious mind would accept that imprint as the desired outcome and move you toward it. If you wish to have more patience with your teenage son, why not rehearse your newfound patience in the theater of your mind? The vivid pictures, sounds, and feelings imprinted by repeated practice would greatly increase the chances of a real performance just like the imagined one. You would become more patient because you've mentally rehearsed what patience is like.

I mentally rehearsed the breaking of the national jump record so often, that when it happened it actually felt familiar; right down to the excited cheering of my family and friends when I skied back to the dock.

Our son, Tyler, was born to play team sports. He spent a few years in competitive water skiing, but gradually moved toward his passion of playing games with a ball. After many years of trying to squeeze all of those sports into each twelve-month period, he settled on baseball upon entering high school. During a game with his summer league team, Tyler struggled at the plate due to a tendency to swing at some high pitches. After striking out, his coach asked him to identify his key thoughts while in the batter's box. Tyler reported that he was thinking about "not swinging at high pitches." (I hope you can see where this is headed!) Coach Sal said, "Let's try focusing on what we want, instead of what we don't want." Then he asked Tyler, "What do you want?" My son replied that he really liked the ball low in the strike zone and down the middle. The coach explained that Tyler needed to spend more time thinking about the pitches he wanted, what they looked like and where they would be. "Replace all other thoughts about various pitches with thoughts of what you want." At Tyler's next bat, much to his surprise, he crushed the ball for a 380-foot homerun. The look on his face as he rounded first base was priceless! Coach Sal was grinning a bit, too.

It amazes me how often we allow ourselves to play in our mind the scenes of things we don't want, or things we dread. We dwell on negative scenes of mistrust, mistakes, misuse, or missed opportunities, instead of disciplining ourselves to focus on positive, productive, peak performing images of how we'd like life to be.

It's your choice. No one else has control of your thoughts. Look in the mirror and meet the writer of your thoughts and the producer of your movie.

How TO <u>Imagine</u> Your Success

I. If this concept is new to you, find a quiet place to sit where you are free from interruptions. Eventually you'll be able to play your movie in the theater of your mind almost anytime you choose.

   Once you're comfortable, close your eyes and imagine a juicy slice of lemon, cut into a wedge and sitting in front of you. Vividly imagine picking up the lemon, bringing it to your mouth and biting into the lemon. Imagine your taste buds reacting to the juice as it flows into your mouth.

   Most people will actually have a physiological experience similar to the real thing! This exercise utilizes the right hemisphere of your brain where your movie theater is stored.

   A second exercise, which will accomplish the same thing, is to imagine a woman standing in front of a class of school children. See her turn toward the chalkboard, raise her arm, and then drag her long fingernails down the chalkboard from top to bottom. Yikes!

   Now you're ready for something more helpful.

II. With your dream and your targets clearly in mind, show yourself a movie in the theater of your mind where you are the star. See the scene as you would see it if it were actually happening right now. However you are not limited by what can be visualized. Imagine the physical sensations of the scene. Imagine the emotions you associate with your scene. Let the sounds, tastes, and smells come to your mind as well. Try to play your movie in "real" time. If for some reason you make a mistake in the execution of some physical act, stop the movie, back it up, and replay that segment with the desired outcome. Hey, it's your movie! You can do it over and over, and anyway you want to.

It's important to experience the movie as if it's actually happening. Lose yourself in it. Play it as many times as seems comfortable or appropriate, but play it perfectly.

III. Repeat often. This exercise should be done daily, at minimum. If you're trying to internalize a new habit or technique, experiencing the scene multiple times per day is extremely helpful.

CHAPTER 7

STEP 4 – BELIEVE

Reprogram Your SELF-Beliefs

If you have a dream and have taken aim on your specific targets, and if you have practiced imagining the desired outcome in advance, there's only one thing that could keep you from achieving your dream... YOU! You, and the silly things you say to yourself, are the only significant obstacles to your success.

Let me use an example to make the point. In some of my workshops I will show my audience a 32-digit number and suggest that everyone take a moment or two to memorize it. Inevitably there are some moans of disbelief and a couple of audible remarks like, "Are you kidding?" I give everyone a few moments during which some people make a real attempt, but most give up and resign themselves to the fact that they can't do it. At this point I take the audience through a story that gives meaning to the number in small bits and pieces. Within three to five minutes I can usually have an audience of any size reciting the entire 32-digit number out loud from memory. I then ask them this question: "What did you hear the small, quiet, little voice in your head say when I asked you to memorize this number?" Most people will admit they heard a voice say things like, "No way" or "I can't do that" or "I'm not good at memorizing." That little voice is the voice of self-talk, and we started hearing that voice regularly around the age of five or six years old. The good news and the bad news is that we tend to believe that voice when we hear it. We think it speaks the truth. In this case, everyone in the audience can usually admit to themselves that the voice in their head was obviously telling them a lie, because they have now memorized the number. And WHY was it possible? Because they found a really good strategy that worked! It wasn't a question of their talents at all!

This brings us to the crucial question for you and your dream. Do you believe in your heart and mind that this dream of yours will definitely become your reality? Is it a done deal in your mind? Can you honestly say that you already know how this story is going to end? When I arrived at the point that I could answer "yes" to all those questions that was the moment when I was truly free to evolve from chump to champ. It represented the moment that I was fully equipped to make my dreams come true. Throughout our lives we'll meet people who do not believe in our dreams. But if WE don't believe in our own dreams, what chance do we have?

You may be wondering, "So what if I don't quite believe it?" When we are short on belief, our commitment is compromised. We protect ourselves by not giving 100% of our time, our energy, or our resources. We've built in a back door for escaping our failure because we can always claim, "Hey I didn't really think it could happen anyway." Total commitment, on the other hand, means all out war on the obstacles blocking your way. Failure (known as quitting) is not even an option. It may take longer than you want, but you know it will be done!

Motivational speakers love to use a story about Cortez to illustrate this point. In 1521, when Cortez was trying to capture the world's greatest treasure from the Aztecs, he supposedly told his men that if they were going home after the great battle, they'd be going home in the ships of the Aztecs. He then ordered his men to burn their own boats to make the point very clear! I guess the men fought surprisingly well the next day. That's what we mean by total commitment and knowing how the story will end! There were no escape routes.

When I ask audiences to look at the four steps of my chump to champ strategy and identify the one step that presents the greatest challenge for them, more than 90% point at "Believing" as the toughest hurdle. Most have some kind of dream. Many can create some goals at which to aim. A few say that they have successfully experienced imagining success, or some kind of mental rehearsal. But almost everyone admits that having absolute, rock solid belief in themselves is very difficult most of the time.

So, why do so many people doubt that they can accomplish their dreams? Why is it that perhaps you don't believe that you can live your dream? The answer is hidden in the example of the 32-digit number. It's because you're repeatedly hearing messages from that small, quiet, little voice in your head that you "Can't do this", or "Aren't good enough for that", or most likely – "It's just too hard." All of us have some of these negative messages rattling around in our head from time to time. Most of our self-talk falls into one of two categories: positive or negative. The positive messages you hear are words of encouragement and praise. The negative messages are words of doubt and criticalness. But where did these messages come from in the first place?

It's probably no surprise to learn that the earliest messages we received about ourselves came from our parents, or those who spent the most time with us. From the very beginning they "accidentally" shaped our self-impressions. I use the term "accidentally" because most parents (but not all) are unaware of how the messages they send to their children get stored and used as if they are facts. If your parents repeatedly used phrases like, "You can do it if you try" and "You certainly are a hard worker" you probably grew up believing you are capable and ambitious. On the other hand, if you repeatedly heard things like, "That's too hard for you; better let me do it" and "You are so lazy; no energy in that body" you grew up believing that you are incapable and inadequate. These are just examples of thousands and thousands of messages sent by our parents, and other influencers, that we internalized, believed, and acted out as if they were true. The real truth is that they were just opinions that we believed (and still believe today) and treated as if they were facts.

Messages like these are similar to software being loaded onto your hard drive, except in this case the hard drive is your brain! Once internalized, the brain runs the software program and we have a self-fulfilling prophecy because you and I will always behave in a way that is consistent with our beliefs (software). If you really believe you are a neat and organized person, you will behave like one. If you really believe you are scatter-brained and disorganized, you will behave that way. What I discovered is that if you really believe you are a national champion water skier – the medal just hasn't arrived yet – you'll behave like one! But if you believe you're just a wannabe champion, you'll behave like that.

What this means is that we must take a hard look at the messages we keep playing in our head, regardless of where they came from and when we got them.

We need to consider the possibility that our mental software – self-beliefs – are not only unhelpful, they're actually holding us back from reaching our dreams!

I call these "Roadblock Beliefs". All of us have some of these. We heard them, adopted them, and now use them to excuse ourselves or explain our mediocrity. Here are some examples:

I'm not very good at staying focused.

I'm lousy at remembering names.

I've never been a quick learner.

I can't control my temper.

I'm not a very patient person.

I'm not creative at all.

I have a lot of problems being self-disciplined.

I've never been good at doing that whole goal-setting thing.

You might think these are harmless or humble comments, but let's look at how these statements undermine your success. When you tell yourself that you're not a patient person, you've given yourself permission to be impatient. The next opportunity you have to show impatience will generate a subconscious thought that says, "Yep, that's just like me" – in other words, it's okay because I'm just being me!

If you've heard yourself say that you're not good at goal setting, then it's easy to explain to yourself and to others why you don't. "Yep, that's just like me" will be your thought when you struggle to set or meet a goal. Every behavior that you see in yourself that matches a self-belief becomes justified, acceptable, and reinforced...but that doesn't mean it's actually a fact. One thing is for sure: it's a Roadblock Belief keeping you from reaching your highest potential.

Let's examine the alternative and its outcome. If I hear myself repeatedly say, "I'm a very focused worker", an image is created in my subconscious that matches. The next time I demonstrate a "focused" behavior, a little voice will jump up and say, "Yep, that's just like me." This serves as a valuable reinforcement to continue showing this behavior. If I believe I'm very self-disciplined – I must be, because I keep hearing myself say it – then it's only natural for my behavior to match the image created by the words. "Yep, that's just like me!" Once again, your subconscious mind does not evaluate your self-talk or judge it as right or wrong. It just accepts it and produces a label for you to believe about yourself.

Who is the final author of your self-talk? It may have been your parents in the beginning, but there comes a time when we must take responsibility for writing our own script. And if you're responsible for writing your own script, why not make it a fantastic script? Do you realize you can change your script today? You can give yourself a mental software up-grade! If you change your messages, you change your world. I know it's hard to believe, but the <u>single most significant</u> difference between you and someone who:

Is good at staying focused,

Is good at remembering names,

Is a quick learner,

Can control their temper,

Is a very patient person,

Is creative,

Is self-disciplined,

Is good at doing that whole goal setting thing, is that they BELIEVE they can. They're running their mental hard drive using different mental software than you are. They are not necessarily more talented than you, or more privileged, more educated, or luckier than you.

Remember, all software is up-gradable!

How TO <u>Believe</u> It Will Happen

I. With your dream, targets, and imagination of success clearly in mind, make a list of as many negative or self-limiting messages you've regularly heard yourself say that might apply. These should be "I" statements that represent the Roadblock Messages of your self-talk.

Examples:

"I'll never get this figured out."

"I'm just not that good at this."

"I'm totally outclassed here."

"I can't do this."

Making the list requires some honest introspection. It may take a few days before you've recognized some of the Roadblock Messages. Because you've heard some of them so often, you might tend to see them as truths instead of the suspicious "software" they really are! Listen to your self-talk carefully to find the messages that need to be up-graded.

II. Since telling yourself to "stop thinking" those thoughts doesn't work, your only hope is to replace the thoughts you don't want. The conscious mind is always thinking something, so give it good healthy things to think!

For every one of your Roadblock Messages, write a new and improved message for yourself. These new messages (soon to be beliefs) must meet the following criteria:

- Begin with "I am; I can; I'm able to; or I do." (Not "I will; I hope to: I'll; or I want to.")
- Be positive, encouraging, and uplifting statements.
- Be stated in the present tense as if they are already true.

Examples:

"I am self-disciplined and able to control my urge to eat junk food."
"I learn new skills easily and have the self-confidence to get past early mistakes."
"I am organized and enjoy using my space and time in a systematic way."
"I am able to meet new people genuinely and form new friendships comfortably."

III. Carry the list of statements with you for the purpose of daily prac-tice. These statements must be said out loud in the beginning, at least three times per day. Eventually they will become part of conscious thought, but only if intentionally practiced at first. Think of how long some of your thoughts have been rattling around on your mental hard drive. To accomplish a successful overwrite, repetition will be required. Hear yourself say the phrase, let it sink in as you internalize its meaning, and then move on to the next phrase. Say each one with confidence, energy, and a strong sense of belief.

Integrating The Four STEPS

It may occur to you as you read this that you've tried setting goals before and didn't get much back in return. Or perhaps you've played particular "happy endings" in your mind on many occasions, but the real world never looked like the movie. You might be thinking that in spite of your best efforts to be a positive person you're still caught up in what Zig Ziglar calls "stinkin' thinkin'. If you've tried some of these strategies and have enjoyed only mediocre results, you're probably thinking, "This stuff doesn't work for me." I want to encourage you to see the four steps as one complete strategy that must be engaged in its entirety. The dramatic transformation that many people experience in their lives is easy for them to understand afterwards, as they look back at how the four steps worked in concert. Having experienced the entire process successfully, it becomes easier to initiate the same process again in another area of life with full confidence about how it will bear fruit once again!

It only makes sense that a great dream is the starting point. But a dream without action remains only a wish. It reminds me of an old Chinese proverb: "Hungry man standing on hill with open mouth waiting for duck to fly in has very long wait."

Even elaborate goals that meet all the criteria can be hindered if your mind is playing movies of mistakes instead of perfection. I was trying to help one of my students who was very inconsistent in slalom skiing competitions. He complained of frequently falling around the fifth buoy (out of a possible six) during tournaments. I asked if he ran a movie of success in his head. He informed me that he ran a mental rehearsal before his event, but that he usually stopped the movie after the fourth buoy because he thought that was good enough! It was good enough for a four buoy performance!

Lastly, great dreams combined with clear targets, backed up with perfect mental movies may still never be realized if you're running software that says "I can't, It won't, and Never will." Believing in the certainty of your story, even before it is a story, has more power than we often comprehend. However, history is filled with stories of people who had huge amounts of self-belief and self-confidence, but lacked the discipline required of a goal setter or the creative power for seeing the outcome in the mind's eye. Bottom line: all four steps must be integrated into the process.

The mathematical chances of successfully transforming any area of your life to a whole new level are exponentially raised when you engage yourself in all four steps of the chump to champ approach. Initially you will take the four steps in sequence, but soon realize that they become integrated steps. On any given day your thoughts will glide seamlessly from the high altitude of your dream down to the earthly details of the day's most immediate target. The moments you steal to play your movie while driving your car (be careful!), exercising, or resting on the couch after a busy day will become automatic and productive. The scenes you imagine will be quietly reinforced with private thoughts like "I am that person; or I can do that." Your life is being transformed because you see your world differently. And because you see your world differently...it is!

> *"The state of your life is nothing more than a reflection*
> *of your state of mind."*
> — *Wayne Dyer, author*

"As I grow older, I pay less attention to what people say.
I just watch what they do." — Andrew Carnegie

SECTION THREE

DO SOMETHING NEW: MAKE A SIGNIFICANT DIFFERENCE

The French poet Molaire once said, "We are alike in the dreams we have and the promises we make to each other; what separates us is what we do." This section places an emphasis on the opportunities you have to distinguish yourself by what you do. There are hundreds and hundreds of moments in a day for you to differentiate yourself from the average person who will most likely respond by: È Choosing the path of least resistance

- Making a choice that makes life more comfortable
- Picking an option that shifts the blame or responsibility

You can be different! You can take the high road, the challenging path, the route that gains the greater good for the greatest number of people, in spite of the difficulties and the risk. By these actions – which only come from those on the "chump to champ" journey – you will have a significant impact on other people and on your organization. That positive impact will cause your personal credibility as a person of influence to soar.

A personal note: There is no tougher proving ground for gaining credibility than with your own children. If it's difficult for you to establish credibility with them, it will be difficult for you in the workplace. If you're doing the right things to earn credibility at home, those same strategies will work for you at work. For this reason you'll find that I use a lot of stories and examples from my parenting experiences. My children have provided me with many life lessons on being believable that can be applied anywhere.

CHAPTER 8

RELY ON MAGNETIC NORTH

If you found yourself lost in the woods on a dark, cold, rainy night, what is the one item you would be lucky to have tucked away in your pocket? While a small morsel of food would be helpful, the only real chance you have of finding your way back to camp is by using a compass.

Consider what information a compass provides, and doesn't provide. It won't tell you where you are – you'd need GPS for that – and it won't tell you where you've been – you'd need a map for that. A compass will tell you only one thing: Magnetic North. However that one piece of information is pivotal, as it becomes the basis for every directional decision. Magnetic North is a reference point that could keep you from making poor choices every time you come to a fork in the pathway.

Believe it or not, you have a built-in compass that offers Magnetic North values for decision-making. These evolved out of the messages you received from your parents and other influencers in your life. The important question is, "When does using this compass have the greatest impact?" The answer is whenever you have crucial choices to make.

Champs rely upon an internal compass to guide their choices in everyday life, and this is why they have followers who trust them. Having an awareness of a personal Magnetic North keeps you from getting lost, or venturing down a road not intended. Larry Smith of Life Coach Today puts it another way. He says, "Live by your values, not by your needs."

Forks in the business pathway present themselves frequently, and the choices you make indicate whether you are using your Magnetic North values consistently, or ignoring them. There are five crucial choices we make everyday. The truest "chump to champ" choices are not always comfortable or without risk. But the long-term benefits will pay huge dividends in your transformation and your credibility.

Are you choosing pathways that coincide with your compass? Are you living by your values or by your needs?

Choice #1

To serve others, or be served by others.

Having others serve you is so flattering! That's why it's so fun to go to a nice restaurant or resort and have the staff members wait on you. Talk about relaxing! However, the irony of the whole scene is that those being served will never feel any better than they do during the very first moment - or first day - of being pampered. Conversely, those who are doing the serving are learning and growing every single moment.

As they learn how to read the needs of their guests they are growing. As they learn different ways to solve guest challenges, they are growing. As they learn to meet the highest needs of those they serve, they are elevated in spirit and in experience. Look for your opportunities to serve those around you. Learn to identify the highest needs of those people and determine what role you can play in meeting those needs. Make it your goal to serve, rather than be served. If you live by your values, you'll recognize other peoples' needs and you'll know what your role could be. If you live by your needs, you'll be looking for someone to take care of you.

Choice #2

To give away power, or grab power for yourself.
Everyone likes the feeling of authority and power. We are control seekers by nature. Therefore it will feel UN-natural for you to give power and authority away when you could keep it for yourself. A great paradox that true champs know is that you gain power when you give it away, assuming

that you give it to those who are ready, able, and willing to receive the authority you give them. Your personal power with those around you will actually increase as they observe you letting go so others may exercise their power. If you live by your values, giving power away makes sense because you recognize it as a growth opportunity for others. If you live by your needs, you will grab power; keep it from falling into the hands of others because you need it to make yourself feel powerful. This is definitely the sign of a chump.

Choice #3

To honor others, or seek to be honored by others.

Like being served in Choice #1, it feels good to be honored. Who wouldn't like to be lifted up in front of their peers or followers to hear the accolades being thrown around? Consequently, chumps tend to look for ways to be honored, or worse, manipulate opportunities to fit their hunger for honors. The tricky thing about honoring is that you can't really successfully do it to yourself! Others must do the honoring, or it isn't honoring…it's boasting and self-promotion. Champs are more concerned with capturing the opportunities for honoring someone else. They understand the importance of honoring someone because of the positive growth in that person's self-esteem and self-image. It's important to have strong partners in the workplace, and one way to strengthen people is to hold a mirror in front of them and help them see the good you see in them. That's what honoring does. If you live by your values, you honor others because of the benefits they receive. If you live by your needs, you miss those opportunities because your eyes are on yourself.

Choice #4

To act out of love, or act out of fear.

James Burke, the CEO of Johnson & Johnson back in the 1980s is a great example. When it was discovered that someone had contaminated Tylenol on the shelves of stores in Chicago, Burke insisted on pulling his product from every shelf in America to insure the safety of the public. It was a very expensive decision for their bottom line; it cost them millions of dollars. But over the long run it led to high praise and high levels of trust for Johnson & Johnson because they did the right thing. The easier, less expensive thing would have been to pull the product only from stores in Chicago, or perhaps statewide. This decision was done out of a love for the customer. It was a decision that overcame the fear of profit loss. What and who do you love? Not in a romantic sense, but in the sense of valuing their worth and being concerned for their well-being. If you live by your values, you will act out of love and concern for someone or something. If you live by your needs, fear of losing something (profit, image, position, or time) will dictate your choice.

Choice #5

To assume the best, or suspect the worst of people and events.

This choice is one of those instant, in-the-blink-of-an-eye kind of reactions. When confronted with information about another person's decision or action, what is your first thought? Is it a thought that assumes the good intentions of this person, or a thought that suspects the worst? Our assumptions about the motives of others are actually a choice we make. Those assumptions say a lot about what we think of their character and their capabilities in general. When people make mistakes, but we assume they are good and well intentioned, our first thought is that the mistake is uncharacteristic – it's "not like them." In this case we separate the doer from the deed and allow them future opportunities. However in a similar situation, if we assume they are either evil or incompetent, our first thought is that this situation is "just like them." The doer and the deed are now one and the same, and they don't deserve another chance. If you live by your values, you believe in human frailty – like your own – and assume the best. If you live by your needs, you suspect the worst about others because it feels personally uplifting to put other people down.

"Be more concerned with your character than your reputation, because your character is what you really are; your reputation is merely what others think you are."
—John Wooden, Hall of Fame Basketball coach

CHAPTER 9

FIND LIFE'S SWEET SPOT

You'll watch the movie less than a minute when you'll hear the line that could change your life. It's a significant bit of wisdom that comes from a dad to his son in "The Natural" starring Robert Redford. While playing catch with young Roy, Mr. Hobbs says, "You have a gift Roy, but it's not enough. You have to develop that gift." In those two short sentences Roy's dad gives us two universal truths, crucial pieces of information about living and about becoming truly outstanding in life. First, YOU have a gift! It sounds like he was speaking to Roy, but he could have been speaking to you! Within you is a gift, a talent, and a natural inclination to excel in some area of life. You are hard-wired to do some things better than others. Some activities just come more naturally for you than they do for other people. The fact that you haven't identified your gift yet doesn't make it any less true. The fact that you doubt the truth of this claim doesn't make it any less true. The existence of your unique gift is a certainty, even if you NEVER look hard enough to find it. It's still there anyway, just undiscovered.

Young Roy knew about the gift to which his father referred. He had a gift for throwing a ball. He had seen and recognized the evidence of this gift. The way he threw the ball when pitching to his dad, was clearly superior to what he'd seen from other boys. He had more velocity, more control, and more movement on his pitches. But if for some reason he did not recognize his gift, and he answered back to his dad, "What gift?" – would that make it any less real? No, the gift would exist anyway. But Roy would not be ready to obey his father's second command to "develop that gift" until he recognized what uniqueness lies within him.

Your sweet spot is similar to the "sweet spot" on a golf club, tennis racket, or baseball bat. The ball travels farther and faster after making contact with that one small area than any other part of the club, racket, or bat. All energy delivered to that spot is magnified exponentially and the rewards are huge. The ball and the striking object were absolutely made for each other, and the results are obvious.

Job #1 for you is to find your life's sweet spot; that place where things come a little easier for you and a little more naturally than for most people. It will be an activity where you learn quickly and make progress with less effort than in other areas of your life where you do not have a gift. Identifying this sweet spot is important because for every moment you spend developing this gift you will enjoy achievement and progress at a greater rate than in other areas. Being well-rounded sounds good in theory, but usually means you are spending time trying to turn a weakness into a strength. The extreme example would be trying to hit a fastball off the handle of the bat. It will fly, but not very far in spite of great effort. It's been said that trying to turn a weakness into a strength is like trying to teach a pig to sing. The entire effort will just make you mad and probably frustrate the pig! If you have a gift for working with numbers, but lack a gift for showing compassion, spend more of your time with numbers than you do with people needing compassion. It's best for everyone!

One of the best books written on the topic is "Now, Discover Your Strengths" by Marcus Buckingham. It includes an opportunity to take an on-line inventory for finding your particular strengths. Buckingham's analogy proposes that we've been dealt some cards to play in life, and cards are like individual gifts or talents. It's just important to realize that no one receives the entire deck of cards, just a handful of cards to play. It means that you are hard-wired to excel in some areas but not in all areas of life. To get the biggest bang for your buck, focus on your strengths and develop your gifts to such a degree that you clearly distinguish yourself. Buckingham's book lists thirty-four different themes as possible gifts. You are a unique blend of these talents. Which ones are yours? In addition to taking a personal inventory like the one mentioned above, consider the following questions.

1. What comes easy for you where some other people struggle?
2. What activity attracts you or gets your attention?

3. What do you enjoy doing, to the point where you look forward to it?

4. What behaviors seem natural or second nature for you?

Having a knack for being organized and focusing on details may be one of your gifts. Physical coordination or being good with your hands is another example. Your gift might be conceptual thinking or strategic planning. Perhaps your competitive nature distinguishes you, or the ability to build relationships quickly. Even high levels of empathy for others could set you apart from the crowd.

Once you find your sweet spot, the next question is where will you use it?

Applying Your Sweet SPOT

Roy Hobbs knew he could throw a ball better than most kids, so knowing where to use that gift was the next question. Sometimes this is called "finding your passion." He might have considered other activities that require the use of a ball – basketball, soccer, even tennis – but it became very clear that baseball was his passion. Roy knew the game of baseball would provide him with the ideal stage upon which to showcase his sweet spot.

Your sweet spot is your gift or your talent. Your passion usually becomes the arena where you get to use it. Your gifts need an outlet. They need an arena in which to find expression. It might be a sport, a particular kind of business, a particular role within a business, or an activity that doesn't pay at all! A passion is something you love to do. In fact you love to do it so much that you'd actually do it for the pure enjoyment of doing it. You find personal fulfillment when you are engaged in this activity.

How will you find your passion? Where will you showcase your sweet spot?

Ask yourself, "What am I doing when I feel the absolute best about me?" "What activities are so satisfying that I can hardly wait until I get to do them again?"

Within the answer to those questions you will probably find your sweet spot and your passion.

I know an eleven-year-old girl who has been blessed with many gifts. She is athletically coordinated, academically disciplined, and theatrically engaging. In addition to being an excellent student, her athletic involvements include running, cycling, swimming, triathlons, and karate. She also often takes a leading role in school and church stage productions. The dilemma she faces is that there is not enough time for all these activities, in spite of the fact that she excels in all of them. It appeared some choices needed to be made for the sake of the family schedule and sanity. One day her mother asked her to rank her enthusiasm for each of the sports she pursues, from one to ten, with ten meaning the highest level of passion. She scored swimming three, cycling and running received a six, and karate carried the day with a seven. As an afterthought, mom asked her daughter what score would she give her drama opportunities. The young girl's face lit up and without hesitation exclaimed, "Oh, that's a ten for sure!" It's not likely any of us would vote to drop an activity where our passion ranks a ten.

What endeavor, activity, or project do you find so engaging that sometimes it keeps you awake at night or stirs you before the alarm goes off? What is it that you can't wait for an opportunity to do again? If you know the answer to these questions, you have found your passion, or at least one of them. Most likely there is a personal sweet spot hidden within it.

Your assignment:

Get a copy of Marcus Buckingham's book, *Now, Discover Your Strengths* and read it.

CHAPTER 10

IDENTIFY AND STAY CLOSE TO YOUR WIZARDS

Wizards are the people in your life who have influence over what you believe to be true. They are people of influence who have some affect on what you accept, versus what you deny, to be reality. Their power comes from the credibility you have assigned to them. Consequently, the older brother you looked up to was a more powerful wizard in your life than the little computer geek living next door because you believed in your brother's wisdom. He was more credible in your eyes. If your brother claimed Willie Mays was the best outfielder in major league history, you would put money on it.

By now you've realized that wizards can be credible in one area and not credible in another. Twenty years after punching out the computer geek for disagreeing with your older brother, you're calling that same computer geek to solve a technical issue regarding your computer. Who's the wizard now? You're not calling your older brother! On a more personal level,

...the most important wizards in your life are the ones who influence what you believe to be true about YOU.

Now that's personal! Your first wizards were your parents. They were credible – or at least started out that way – because they were your parents. They were the first ones to help you shape your opinion of "you." Parents have "box seats" when it comes to influencing the beliefs of young children. If they continuously reinforced the idea that you were neat, tidy, orderly, and clean – you believed it, and acted accordingly. If, on the other hand, they regularly sent the message that you were sloppy, messing, disorderly, and unkempt – you believed that instead, and acted accordingly.

For this reason, the Great Oz in *The Wizard of Oz* captures our attention so easily. Dorothy and her friends believe in the power of the Wizard to such an extent that they will do whatever he asks of them. He has a lot of credibility. While it's true that he momentarily loses that credibility when they learn of his charade, he regains enough credibility to give each character the belief they need to fulfill their dreams. It's the reassurance of the Wizard that causes the Cowardly Lion to say, "I have courage!" It's the Wizard's affirmation that leads to Tin Man's claim, "I have a heart!" Even the Scarecrow believes a new truth about himself due to the influence of the Wizard.

Who are the wizards in your life today? Who are the individuals helping shape your beliefs about who you are? Can you identify your wizards? Some wizards are in formal positions like our teachers, preachers, coaches, and mentors. Others might be close personal friends, work associates, recreation teammates, or relatives. It all comes down to whose opinion really matters to you; whose opinion of you do you long to hear? If you really care what a particular person sees in you, he or she is a potential wizard.

Here's an equally important question: Are your wizards positive or negative? That's right – they come in two flavors! Positive wizards are the people whose observations of you, and words about you, always lift you up. When the words of a wizard make you feel good about yourself, or help you see your strengths, you are in the presence of a positive wizard. Stay close! Positive wizards see the potential that's locked inside you and help you know it's there. They paint a positive and encouraging picture for you of the person you will become. It's a message of hope. We need them for just that reason, because it's hard to see a picture of yourself when you're in the frame!

Negative wizards will seldom admit that they are negative, but the recipients of their work know it's true. The power of a negative wizard should never be underestimated. Negative wizards are indeed still wizards because of the credibility you have assigned them. They are the people in your world that send depressing or gloomy messages to you about your future. They will call it "being realistic," not negative. You will recognize the presence of a negative wizard by the self-doubt you feel about yourself or your future. There is absolutely no benefit to associating with this kind of wizard. Run, don't walk, as fast as you can in another direction. At the very least, tell yourself that the product they are selling is not for you!

At the age of ten, my daughter turned in one of her best slalom skiing performances of the year while competing at the U.S. National Water Ski Championships. However, as she completed her run, she fell and struck her forehead on the tip of the ski while trying for one more buoy. By the time she swam to shore a remarkable goose egg had appeared on her forehead along with a flood of tears. She had one more event to ski that day – the trick skiing event – and the overall title for her division was up for grabs. I knew she could win it if she turned in a good trick score. Approximately two hours later, our daughter sat on a towel with three of her competitors near the starting dock waiting her turn for the final event. As she prepared she held a small ice bag to her forehead in an effort to reduce the swelling. In the midst of the small talk between the girls, one of them noticing the still-prominent goose egg quipped, "Well, it just isn't your day." I overheard the comment and immediately recognized the presence of the negative wizard. She was indeed a wizard because she had won many events in the past. The question in my mind was whether my daughter would buy in to the wizardry – after all, her injury gave her a perfect excuse for a sub-par performance – or, would she reject it?

In a split second I saw her head snap around and look at the other young girl. "Oh, yes it is!" came the reply. I quietly clapped as I turned and walked away. She went on to win the event that day and the overall title. To this day, I know the victory was won while sitting on the beach, long before her ski hit the water. It happened when she rejected the forecasting of a negative wizard.

Your assignment:

Find your positive wizards and make a list of their names. Spend time with them and internalize their messages of hope about your value and your future. Reject the messages of negative wizards and develop strategies for minimizing your contact with them.

The final step is to ask yourself, "For whom am I a wizard?" And, "In what way can I play my role more effectively?"

CHAPTER 11

GET COMFORTABLE WITH BEING UNCOMFORTABLE

Human beings are comfort seekers. They frequently choose the path of least resistance or the easiest way to do most things rather than the best way. Observe your own behavior and you'll see what I mean. You sit in your car at a fast-food drive-thru despite a very long line, even if the line is shorter inside the restaurant. Why? Because it's faster or because it's easier? Probably because it's less effort and more comfortable. If you're like most Americans, you spend most or all of your monthly income – and perhaps a little more on credit. Why? Because it's better or because it's easier than budgeting and saving? Probably because it's easier and makes life more comfortable. If you cook at home using frozen foods rather than cooking from scratch, ask yourself why. Is it because it's better for you, or because it's easier? Probably because it's easier.

Lastly, think about what happens at work. When a major change in procedure is proposed, do you immediately think of ways to implement it, or do you think of ways to argue against it? If you argue against it, is it because the argument is superior to the change, or because defeating the change is easier than embracing and adjusting to it?

After all, change is uncomfortable, and that's why most people fight it – to avoid the feelings of discomfort.

Here's the irony. Most people accept the idea intellectually that they must change in order to grow. They accept the notion that giving up the old is necessary before the new can be experienced and appreciated. But the feeling of being uncomfortable during the change is so against their nature, that emotions win the battle and comfort is preferred. Some of the classic battles of human behavior illustrate this. To quit smoking is very uncomfortable, both physically and emotionally, yet who would argue against the benefits? So why do we still have so many people smoking? Most likely they are not willing to endure the period of time when they will be uncomfortable. To lose weight is also very uncomfortable. Everyone admits to the logic and the benefits – socially and medically. But the discomfort of self-discipline, food management, and exercise will discourage most and leave them voting for the comfort of the status quo.

With every great step of personal growth, or personal change, there will be a period of discomfort.

When a baseball player attempts to steal second base, there is a period of time during which he is very uncomfortable. It is that time when he has the security of neither first base nor second base. It's very uncomfortable! But it must be endured to have something new. Hence the saying by author Burke Hedges, "You can't steal second base with your foot on first."

Your journey to new skills, new habits, new opportunities, or new appearances, will require you to get uncomfortable. You must actually get comfortable with being uncomfortable. This means you must embrace the feeling of discomfort and re-label it as a good thing! It is a period of transition that precedes the very thing you want for yourself.

Learning a new skill like public speaking usually means suffering through the embarrassment and frustration of poorly executed attempts before standing in front of an audience begins to feel natural. It's uncomfortable, but well worth the price! Developing a new habit like exercising regularly means the discomfort of fitting it into your schedule and feeling like you're wasting valuable time. Those feelings will eventually give way to a kind of positive anticipation before a workout and euphoria afterwards. Even a new social or business opportunity will carry with it the uncomfortable feelings of anxiety, insecurities, and self-doubt. For some people, that discomfort is so unacceptable they would rather pass on a life-changing opportunity.

Look for places in your life where you can actually practice doing something that makes you uncomfortable. Experience and accept the discomfort as normal and healthy. The nervousness you feel is a human reaction designed to heighten your senses and make you aware that you are in transition. It's the only way for you to truly move from chump to champ. The caterpillar does it when it transforms itself into a butterfly – you can, too.

Your assignment:

As a test, try some new things like buying different brands of products than you normally use at home. Choose a completely different route to drive to and from work for a week. Call a friend that you seldom call and get together socially. Try a recreational activity that you've never tried. Purchase a type of book you never buy (romance, mystery, biography, business book) and make yourself read it. Challenge yourself with experiences that make you a little uncomfortable so you become more comfortable with being uncomfortable!

When you find ways to experience that uncomfortable feeling, jot down some notes about how you felt before, during, and after. Ask yourself to stretch, and expect the new you to begin to appear. There is a struggle going on in the midst of the battle for personal growth, and you must agree to take part in the struggle. It will be uncomfortable, but it will be worth it.

> *"Adversity has the effect of eliciting talents, which, in prosperous circumstances, would have lain dormant."*
> *—Horace*

CHAPTER 12

NOT FEELING LIKE IT? DO IT ANYWAY

By the time our daughter Tarah was twelve, it was common to see her writing down specific water skiing goals on colored paper with an artistic flair. Some goals were short-term performance targets, while others looked much further out at specific outcomes like making the U.S. Team.

We awoke one particular Saturday morning to find the weather windy, overcast, and nasty. The lake was rough, but not too rough to ski; the air was unseasonably cool, but not too cold to ski. I knew it wouldn't be pleasant, but we were planning on a good day of practice. I announced that I'd go down to the lake and get the boat ready. Tarah's reply to this was, "Dad, I don't really feel like skiing today." I said, "I understand. I'll go get the boat ready." She looked surprised and said again, "It's nasty out there, and I really don't feel like practicing." To which I again replied, "I know, you're right. I'll go get the boat ready." By then she was really frustrated and wondering if I had heard a thing she'd said. "Dad! Don't you get it? I don't feel like it!" Finally it was time to make the point. "Tarah, it's perfectly fine that you don't feel like skiing, but what does that have to do with it? Let's do it anyway."

I went on, knowing there was some risk involved, "You've stated your goals and plotted your course for reaching them. There will be many days when you don't feel like doing the work, but go ahead and do it anyway." I went on to add, "Feeling like it, is not a pre-requisite. It's theoretically possible to not feel like it all the way to a national record, if you're willing to do the work!"

Doing the hard things is often accompanied with "not feeling like it." However, true champions are people who are willing to do the hard things despite their feelings at the moment. If you always wait until you feel like doing some things, they will probably never get done! Digging down deep within yourself to do the things that must be done is the essence of self-discipline. The alternative looks easier, and therefore attractive, but actually includes a heavier price in the long run. Author Jim Rohn wrote, "We must all suffer from one of two pains: the pain of discipline or the pain of regret. The difference is discipline weighs ounces while regret weighs tons."

Now that you've committed yourself to a chump-to-champ journey, examine your average day or week and identify the situations or opportunities that require you to do the hard things. What are they? Here are some examples.

- Completing the paperwork following a sale or agreement.
- Phone calls to prospects.
- Speaking in front of a group of your peers.
- Speaking in front of a group of any kind.
- Attending large social gatherings.
- Meeting strangers and engaging in small talk conversations.
- Opening up with friends to expose true feelings on a subject.
- Confronting someone over a behavior issue.
- Listening to feedback about your work.
- Tackling long tedious or repetitive projects.
- Practicing a new skill until perfected.
- Organizing people for a project.
- Organizing the details for an event.
- Reading an entire book related to your field.
- Writing a report.
- Studying data and making sense of it.
- Sticking to a schedule.
- Sticking to a budget.
- Following the rules.
- Standing in a long slow-moving line for something.

The secret to not feeling like it and doing it anyway is to discover the "psychic income" you receive.

Those who are good at doing the painful, distasteful things will tell you that there is a pay-off that is experienced internally. It is a satisfaction on a psychological level that feels rewarding and fulfilling. Be prepared for the natural tug-of-war that will rage within you as you face the hard things you'd rather avoid. Part of you wants to run away or find something easier to do until this hard thing goes away. But the part of you that says, "I don't feel like, but I must" is the part worth listening to. Will yourself to do the things others won't do and you'll have the things others won't have.

The gains for the pain are the feelings of well-being for having done the hard thing, rather than running or hiding from it. Your psychic income is immediate, and therefore a reinforcement for doing it again. The long-term gains are best described not by what you get, but by what you become – self-disciplined!

Your assignment:

Find a copy of Kent Keith's book, *Anyway, The Paradoxical Commandments* and read it for more insights on why we can, and must, do the hard things.

Find and read a copy of John F. Kennedy's speech from September 12, 1962, when he provided the students at Rice University with the primary reason that the U.S. should land a man on the moon by the end of the decade.

CHAPTER 13

TAKE CONTROL

I'll never forget the day it happened. I'm referring to the day my eighteen-year-old son let me know that I was not in control of his baseball career or training, and he was! Actually, that transition had happened over a period of time, but this was the day I realized the cold hard truth of it all. It just so happens that I was the last one to get the memo! We were at the batting cage and he was hitting off a pitching machine while I observed.

After a few swings I began sharing my observations – mostly positive – about what I was seeing in his swing. He was very quiet. When I started suggesting that he change something about his bat position, he let the bat barrel drop to the ground, leaned on it while he delivered his message. "Dad, I know what I'm doing, and what I'm doing is fine.

I've got it, okay?"

At first, I was a little offended. After all, I was the one who taught him which hand goes in the glove, how to throw, and how to swing. I'd been his personal coach since he was four years old. I thought, "Who does he think he is, ignoring my brilliant and helpful advice?" Out loud I muttered something about "Only trying to help" and "I know what I'm seeing here."

Again, he calmly reminded me, "Dad, I know what I'm doing and I don't want the help right now. In fact, I'm beginning to tune you out." Ouch, that hurt. We both got quiet for another whole round of pitches from the machine. He continued swinging away, probably not concentrating all that well due to the distant look on my face. I pondered his words until I had my own little "aha!"

When he finished he looked at me and asked, "Are you mad?" I surprised him with my answer. "No, not at all. I'm sure I arrived at the same place with my dad one day when I announced to him, 'I've got it now.'" I went on, "There comes a time when you're meant to take control of your game, your plan, your strategy. It's yours to control and it needs to be that way. I'm happy for you!" We hugged and he looked very relieved.

Have you taken control of your game yet? Many professionals have not. They continue to look around wondering who's going to give them a plan. Who's going to show them the way? They're still wondering what's going to happen to their career, as if the decision belongs to someone else!

Do you remember when you were a child and you fell down and scraped your knee. You stayed down on the ground and waited for Mom to come running. You just knew she would come. "Is Mom coming?" you asked. Well here's a news flash for you regarding your career today: NO ONE'S COMING!

You are responsible for your plan, your strategy, and your game and no one's coming. As long as you wait as if someone is coming to help you, there will be a strong tendency for you to place blame in every direction. You'll start blaming your manager for not giving you enough training or support. You'll blame your supervisor for not giving you the right assignment. You'll blame your wife and family for demanding too much attention. You might even blame your parents for not getting you the right kind of education. These serve only as excuses for you not taking control.

At some point the blame game must stop and you must take control of your career and your future. Even if you must wrestle it away from someone...

...as my son did...

take sole responsibility for your direction and your success.

As you take ownership and feel a sense of being your life's project manager, ideas and resources will begin to appear to help you. Solutions to some of your biggest questions will find their way to your desk.

This doesn't mean you have to go it alone. You are the architect and project manager of your story, but you can choose the "sub-contractors" (coaches, mentors, advisors, and counselors) to insure the safe completion of the project. Build your dream team of believers in the form of other professionals and friends who can support your journey. I recently secured the services of a "life coach" to help me see my strengths and opportunities, both personally and professionally. However, there is still one prevailing parameter – it's my story and therefore my responsibility to make my decisions and take charge of the implementation of those decisions.

One word of caution is due here. You were meant to assume responsibility for the pathways of your choice and the destination of your heart. To do this you will need to take control of your career's journey, but only by controlling the things you can control – which means "you."

Have you ever witnessed someone who has taken control of everything and everyone, all in the name of reaching their personal goals? Let's be reasonable. Somewhere between blaming everyone else while you do nothing, and controlling everyone else so you can have what you want, there's an intelligent and responsible posture that helps foster team success while you're on the way to personal achievement. Champs are great leaders and facilitators of the other success stories around them. They bring a lot of winners with them on their way to fulfillment. They know that whatever serves the greater good will ultimately serve them as well.

Your assignment:

On a scale of one (low) to ten (high), to what degree have you taken control (read: taken personal responsibility for your plan) in the areas of:

Your health?

Your family life?

Your career growth?

Your financial status?

Your social opportunities?

Your emotional maturity?

Your spiritual development?

"Somewhere along the line of our development we discover what we really are, and then we make our decision for which we are responsible. Make that decision primarily for yourself because you can never live anyone else's life."

—Eleanor Roosevelt

CHAPTER 14

THOU SHALT NOT JIVE THYSELF: LOOKING IN THE MIRROR

Ignaz Semmelweis was an obstetrician at Vienna's General Hospital in the mid-1800s. This particular hospital was an important research hospital as well as the primary health facility at the time. Dr. Semmelweis had responsibilities for research on cadavers as well as delivering babies. He was perplexed by the high mortality rate of his maternity ward where one in ten women died giving birth. Imagine the fear most women faced as they went to the hospital to have their babies!

Semmelweis examined and monitored all the protocols and procedures trying to determine the cause. He noticed that a second maternity ward staffed by midwives had a much lower mortality rate, but could not determine the reason.

A startling clue presented itself. Semmelweis left Vienna for a four-month leave to visit another hospital. When he returned he discovered the mortality rate had improved dramatically in his absence. Suddenly, Semmelweis had to ask himself some really tough questions. What part did he play in this dreadful disease, which had come to be known as childbed fever? When he realized that the primary difference between his work and the work of the midwives was that he spent time working on cadavers, and they did not, Semmelweis developed his theories about the existence of germs. Up to this point, all of medicine focused its attention on symptoms, and nothing was known of germs. Semmelweis determined that tiny diseased particles were being carried from the cadavers to the healthy patients on the hands of the doctors, without them being aware of it. Once a hand-washing policy was implemented for all those attending to patients, the death rate fell to one in a hundred!

Think of the impact on Semmelweis when he had to face the implications of his blind spot, his own contribution to the death rate. It was only when he reached the point of asking the most incriminating question of all did he find the true answer.

Self-deception is a very human and a very common reality. You can minimize similar scenarios in your life if you're willing to ask, "What part of this situation is caused by me?" Asking this question is not as effortless as it might seem. You were encouraged from a very early point in your life to be "right" rather than "wrong." Your parents let you know that they were right and you were wrong and then urged you to find ways to be more right. When you entered school, the teacher rewarded people for having right answers, not wrong answers. It was always more cool to be right with your friends. In fact, winning an argument meant you were right and someone else was wrong.

The problem is that we place such a premium on being right that we lose the humility and the ability to consider the possibility of being wrong! Consequently, we feel an urge to look anywhere but at ourselves to find the cause of our problems.

We blame, we finger point, and we excuse ourselves, when in fact we need to look in the mirror and ask the question: "What part of this is mine?"

The purpose of asking such open, soul-searching questions is that it broadens your view and perspective on any situation. Asking the questions gives you the opportunity to think, to reflect, and to consider new possibilities. Here are some examples of things to ask yourself. These questions are not meant to heighten your paranoia, but are designed to help you consider your role in misunderstandings, conflict, and troubled relationships.

In what way did I add confusion to this situation?

How did I miss-communicate my real intentions?

In what way did I offend him/her?

What have I done to create mistrust?

How have I contributed to anyone's intimidation or fear?

What impression did I create during that encounter that is not accurate?

There are other types of questions to ask yourself that raise your game from chump to champ. Good questions, even when you ask them of yourself, draw consideration and thoughts from deep within you. Your subconscious knows the answers to many of your concerns, but it's not until you actually hear yourself ask, that you will hear yourself answer! Usually, the answers are very revealing and will provide direction for your next move. Here are some examples.

What are my top ten strengths?

What are my top ten opportunities for improvement?

What gives me the most joy in my life?

What causes me the most anxiety in my life?

What one area of my life is most out of balance (not up to speed) with the other areas? How can I adjust to bring it into balance?

Which relationship in my life needs the most attention at this time? What can I do about it?

I've been saving one of the best questions for last. Here it is: "How can I see this situation differently?" When our daughter Tarah was twelve or thirteen, she became fascinated with make-up and hairstyles and all the things you would expect of a young girl that age. Most Sunday mornings I sat in the car with the rest of the family impatiently waiting and waiting for her to make her appearance so we could leave and arrive at church on time. Week after week we were late in spite of my various attempts to make it very clear the exact time I planned to exit the garage! I was getting extremely frustrated and began to view this tardiness as disrespect for *my* schedule and *my* authority. My feelings toward her lateness manifested themselves in sarcastic comments and scowling stares as she approached the car each Sunday morning. Then it occurred to me that my response to the situation had actually become part of the problem. I was always angry by the time we got to church. How ironic is that? My wife helped me find the right question to ask myself. She said, "Do you really think this is about disrespect, or could it be something else?" Knowing that Tarah had never shown deliberate disrespect, I had to consider the possibility that I had to look at this differently. My wife intuitively knew the answer. (But hey, she's a woman and went through this stage herself. That's an unfair advantage!) This whole little drama was because my daughter's number one priority was to look her best. It had nothing to do with me! I had turned it into a battle of wills, when in fact she just needed more time, now that eye shadow and lip-gloss had entered our lives. I was blind to the truth until I changed the question from "Why won't people do differently?" or, "What else is going on here that I'm missing?"

The answers to your questions will serve you best if you write them down, and then look for other possible questions that need asking. When you have the right ones, ask the questions out loud, listen to your internal answers and begin writing. As you write, more and more will be revealed to you. Some people call this journaling. What you call it is less important than taking the time to do it. You have some really good answers locked inside you, just waiting for a really good question to be asked. Ask it!

Your assignment:

Identify a situation or a relationship in your life where you are not pleased with your outcomes. Ask yourself, "What part of this situation am I responsible for? What have I done to add to this?" Write out the answers you hear in your mind. Be completely honest with yourself!

CHAPTER 15

HEAD FOR THE HIGH GROUND: NO EXCUSES

O f all the things you might do to be more champ than chump, this one thing will be so noticed, so distinguishing, and so revealing of your stature, that people will stop and stare with open jaw. The reason for this startled response is that this one action is so rare today that when someone displays it, all conversation is halted out of awe. Old school calls it "taking responsibility." Some call it "owning up." Conners, Smith, and Hickman call it "operating above the line" in their book, *The Oz Principle*. Younger people just say, "My bad." Whatever phrase you prefer, it's definitely the high ground in the battle for credibility.

I'm talking about exercising your choice to take ownership (responsibility) for your actions, rather than offer up excuses. People have been dodging responsibility for thousands of years, so the urge to do so is understandable! Most of the time excuses seem perfectly normal to those who use them because they represent "the reasons why it happened." The teller of the story sees himself as a victim. Excuses are used to explain away the mistake, error in judgment, or poor execution, and basically claim "not my fault." But those who hear "the reason why" don't actually hear "reasons," they only hear excuses, which are not very appealing. And yet, this approach is so commonly used.

If you are truly interested in heading for the high ground there are two things you need to know. First, the bad news: The air is thin up there. By that, I mean this is not a challenge for the faint of heart. It's very difficult to do consistently. Second, the good news: There's very little competition *because* the air is thin up there! If you can make this transition in your personal and professional life, you'll be one of the few with a bird's eye view!

Here's a real life example of how the low road compares to the high ground. I was giving a workshop in Dallas for a large corporation. All employees received specific instructions about time, location, and the need to be on time for the morning session. Two gentlemen arrived late: one about twenty minutes and the other about thirty minutes after we had started. Individually, they came up to see me during our morning break. The first one said, "I want to apologize for being late. The traffic was really bad today." I thanked him for his apology. The second gentleman walked up and said, "I want to apologize for being late today. The traffic was really bad and I should have left my house much sooner today." While these two responses might sound similar, there is a monumental difference in the message behind the words. The first response says, "I'm a victim due to the traffic, which I have no control over, so don't blame me." The second response says, "I'll take ownership for being late, because I realize I had control over what time I left my house, and I could have done better."

Playing the victim will always be attractive to those who specialize in excuses. It sounds good, you think you look better, and it feels like it's an easy way to escape the blame. But the sad truth is that this strategy makes you look powerless and weak to those around you. I heard a woman claim, "I can't help it that I'm late. I got a speeding ticket! It's not my fault he pulled me over and made me late." This kind of thinking is so pervasive in our "blame-game" society that many people have lost sight of how irresponsible they've become. Denial, finger pointing, and excuse offering is so common that when someone stands up to say, "That was my fault" most observers are stunned. Looking at the world stage, President John F. Kennedy's speech in which he took personal responsibility for the failure of the Bay of Pigs invasion in 1961 (Cuba) stands as one of the few times in modern history where a world leader was not seen ducking for cover after a failure. His popularity with the American public didn't miss a beat.

The greatest temptation faced by leaders today is to appear seven-feet tall and bulletproof to their followers. To be perfect, flawless, and invincible seems like the ideal image for some leaders.

Perhaps you might even wonder, "Why would anyone follow me if I'm flawed and vulnerable? Isn't perfection the goal?" Actually, being honest is the goal.

We admire people who show us true humility. We admire the transparency of someone being vulnerable enough to say, "I blew it," apologizing for mistakes or poor judgments. Have you ever noticed the look of relief – and maybe surprise – on your children's faces when you apologize for a mistake or acknowledge poor judgment? Your coworkers may have the same surprise at first. But once they learn that you are a person who takes personal responsibility for your decisions – especially if it includes an apology – your credibility will soar in their eyes.

The next sign of someone heading for the high ground is a commitment to fix what's broken. Once you own it, declare your solution or find one. Identify the root cause of the problem, and then own the answer as well. I recently heard about an employee who was constantly late for work because she kept sleeping through her alarm. She admitted the problem was her responsibility. However, when asked for a solution by her supervisor, she suggested that the supervisor call her house each morning at 6:30 AM to make sure she got up! Taking responsibility means more than just admitting and apologizing. It means solving the issue at hand to eliminate a repeat performance.

While I consulted for a fine-dining restaurant in Central Florida, I met a part-time worker who serviced the bar area in the evenings after classes. She admitted to me that she had a built-in "ownership" device in her head. She said, "If I'm walking anywhere in the restaurant and my eyes catch a glimpse of something out of place – trash on the floor, silverware missing from a table, or chairs misplaced – I own it, and I must fix it. I can't just walk on by. If I see it, I own it." Now that's taking responsibility!

The difference between the low road and the high ground becomes more obvious when you hear the language that goes with each one.

Chump/Victim	Champ/Responsible
"I don't see it as a problem."	"There's an opportunity here."
"It's not my fault."	"I am responsible."
"It's because of…"	"I will find a solution."
"Someone else should have…"	"It belongs to me."
"I did all I could."	"I will do better next time."

Your assignment:

Listen carefully to your speech for three days, taking note of any instances when you offer justification for your actions that make you sound like a victim. Look for phrases that equate to "not my fault," "someone else's fault," or "no one told me what to do." Then write down what you could have said that would show more personal responsibility for your actions.

CHAPTER 16

CHOOSE BETWEEN COULD
AND COULD NOT

A friend of mine, who is an avid cyclist, introduced me to the world of cycling, long distance riding, and road racing. As you can imagine, hill climbing on a road bike requires both stamina and leg strength. We were discussing why some riders are frequently first at the top of the hill. I had noticed that those riders are often in the middle of the pack at the bottom of the hill, or even halfway up, but then pulled away during the last half of the hill. My friend Jim instructed me this way. "Strong riders know the right time and the right place on the hill to use their strength. They could exert themselves at the bottom of the hill, but they know that might turn out to be a foolish use of their energy if the goal is to be first at the top, so they save it for the right time." Then he added the line that had the greatest impact, "Just because you can, doesn't mean you should." Jim was letting me know I always had a choice. I could, or I could not.

Cycling on the road, like any other journey, consists of a lot of choices. To go fast, or go slow is a choice. To follow someone, or to pass is a choice. To "attack" for the lead, or remain a follower is a choice. To obey the traffic signs, or run red lights is a choice. Freedom of choice is a wonderful thing, if you know what you're doing.

When you don't know what you're doing, or appear uncertain, you will always find people who want to tell you what you should do. They will tell you that you should go faster, or you should go slower. They'll advise that you should be more assertive, or that you should not have spoken up. There's no end to the list of things they believe you should do. Parents are particularly good at "shoulding," which is a subtle way of saying "shame on you" for doing or not doing something they want. It's no mystery why you hear your own inner voice telling you that you should stand up for yourself, or you should lose weight, or you should demand more money. In those cases, you're saying "Shame on me!" This can't be good. There must be a better way.

Victor Frankl, in his book *Man's Search for Meaning*, asserted that the one freedom that cannot be taken from you is the freedom to choose how you will react to any situation and to any person. What would your life be like if all the shoulds were removed? How would you feel if you were left with the one true freedom to choose between "I could" and "I could not"? No shoulds!

Think of the ownership you would have and the satisfaction you would have, if you recognized and accepted that you could choose to do something or you could choose not to do something. You are free to choose cheating on your income tax....I could.... or, I could choose not to cheat. There are no shoulds! Now, what do you choose? You could stop at the red light or you could not stop at the red light. You could remain calm during an argument, or you could not remain calm.

What do you choose?

When all choices are based on "what should you do," you become dependent on the opinions of others and what you've been told you should do. If this is the case, is the choice really yours?

When you choose between what you could or could not do, your decision can be based on the single most important criteria...the consequences of your choice!

The decision must be yours because the consequences are certainly going to be yours! No one else gets to endure or enjoy the consequences of your choices, in spite of all the shoulds you've heard.

When an athlete is considering a choice between training in lousy weather or taking the day off, it's a choice between "I could" and "I could not." A good decision will be based upon the possible consequences, and the thinking might go like this (with the consequences underlined).

"The practice in this weather will be <u>good for my skills</u>."

"The practice in this weather might be <u>bad for my health</u>."

"I'll <u>gain some ground</u> on my competition who will certainly take to-day off."

"I will definitely <u>be uncomfortable</u> training in this weather."

The coach, or mom and dad, might be saying, "You should practice to-day" or "You shouldn't practice today." However, they won't experience the consequences; you will! Real freedom of choice is when the athlete considers the consequences of his or her choice by asking the ultimate question. "What will I become by practicing or not practicing today?"

When you choose to lose your temper in an argument, what are your consequences?

When you choose to cheat on an exam, what are your consequences?

When you choose to show respect to a co-worker, what are your consequences?

When you choose to take an extra moment to do a thorough job, what are your consequences?

In each case, the point is you have a choice; you could, or you could not. Just know that your choice dictates not only what you will get, but also what you will become as a person. Every choice has consequences. Let that knowledge guide your decision, and you'll find that you are truly free.

<u>Your assignment:</u>

Identify at least three clear and critical choices you have in front of you to-day. Recognize each choice and the probable corresponding consequences that will come from each one. Write out the consequences on paper.

Refuse to let yourself use the word "should" as you make your choice. Think of yourself as free to choose, and then make your choice based upon the consequences you prefer.

CHAPTER 17

LOOK FOR LESSONS EVERYWHERE

Liz Allen was the dominant woman water skier of the 60s and 70s. In 1969, she won the slalom, trick skiing, and jump event at the National Championships, Masters, and World Championships, a feat almost without parallel in any sport. She had an incredible career that included three overall world championships and eight individual world event titles.

I spent one entire winter training with Liz after her retirement, and one particular incident sticks in my mind. After returning from the lake and a day of practice, Liz asked me for a report on how things had gone during my sessions. I reported that it was a bleak day and that I had several bad ski rides. She looked at me and said, "That's too bad. I never had a bad ski ride." I looked at her with disbelief! I was thinking to myself, "Okay, you were good, but you weren't that good! Everyone has bad days." Having read my mind, she responded. "Oh, I had some ski rides that were not as good as others, but I never allowed myself to label them as bad. There was always something worthwhile in every ride and I would look for it until I could claim it as the one good thing I learned during that ride." I quickly realized how this strategy set her up for having an even better session the next ride. In my case, I would frequently carry negative baggage from one "bad" ski ride to the next, thereby creating a string of lousy sessions!

Years later as I watched my son or daughter struggle in a practice or a game situation, I adopted the practice of asking them one important question: "What did you learn; what were the lessons?" At first, the emotions of striking out in a baseball game or falling in the lake on an easy trick seemed to block all thinking. But after a while, it became a healthy habit to focus more on the lessons learned than on the frustrations of the event.

Life and business are full of lessons for us to use if we'd just take the time to look for them. Every encounter with a co-worker that includes a conversation that didn't go well has a lesson hidden within it. What did you learn? Every call to a prospective customer has a lesson in it; the ones that fail to advance the sale and the ones that do! What did you learn? When Alex Rodriquez hits a homerun, he also looks for the lesson. What worked?

Think of all the opportunities you have to look for lessons in the average day. Do you really have bad days? Or, do you have days full of lessons? When you label a day as a bad day, are you referring to things out of your control, or are there incidents within your control where a lesson has not yet been learned?

When a lesson is not learned, life has a way of re-enrolling you in the class all over again!

Hence, the same mistake is made over and over until the lesson is learned. Then, and only then, the next lesson can be learned.

We have lessons to learn in our relationships. There are lessons to learn about managing life emotionally, physically, and spiritually. There are administrative and organizational lessons. There are career lessons, business lessons, and lessons in leadership. Most important is grasping the concept of lesson learning because those who do not just continue to make the same mistakes over and over.

Here are some sample questions to ask yourself when things do not turn out as well as you'd like.

What just happened?
What did I experience or receive?
How was it different from what I expected or hoped for?
What part was within my control?
What could I have done differently to get a different result?
What will I do differently next time?
So, what have I learned?

What is the alternative to all this learning, besides repeated mistakes? When learning is not happening something else takes its place. The opposite of learning is not unlearning, but judging. When you fail to ask questions like the ones above, you are more likely to spend your time casting judgments on yourselves and others. This shifts the blame and avoids the learning opportunity. Here are some examples using the questions from above.

Learning	Judgments
What just happened?	That should not have happened to me.
What did I experience or receive?	I must be bad since that happened to me.
How was it different from my expectations?	I should get what I want.
What part was within my control?	"They" were wrong to do this to me.
What could I have done differently to get a different result?	"They" should have done it the way I wanted.
What will I do differently next time?	"They" need to change.
What have I learned?	This is bad or wrong.

The first instinct for most people, unfortunately, is to cast a judgment. It takes a moment longer to decide to look for the lesson, rather than jump to a judgment. This approach can become a healthy habit. Imagine yourself getting turned down for a particular role at work, losing a sale to an inferior competitor, or being rejected by a friend. Each of these is emotionally charged and will result in some pain or a sense of loss. However, in each case there is also a lesson to be learned and the sooner you begin to search for the lesson, the sooner the event will begin to make sense to you.

Remember, there is no such thing as failure, only lessons. However, when you do not learn one of life's lessons, you can look forward to a repeat performance!

<u>Your assignment:</u>

Write a list of the top five lessons you have learned recently at work or home.

Write a list of the top two *work* and top two *home* situations with which you are faced right now that seem to be potential lesson givers.

CHAPTER 18

SAY IT WITH YOUR BODY

I t was the championship game between two Little League rivals. The Bulldogs had gone undefeated throughout the season while the Lions had the second-best record with two loses. The Bulldogs chose their starting pitcher based on who threw the ball the hardest. The Lions chose their pitcher based on who would remain most calm under pressure, even if his throwing velocity was not the fastest. It didn't take long for the wisdom of the strategies to be revealed. In the first inning, with a runner on base due to a nice single, one of the Lions launched a bomb to deep centerfield for a homerun and a two-run lead. He was the most respected hitter in the lineup, and this hit was seen as a forecast by the Bulldog's pitcher. With that one hit, the body language of the young pitcher changed dramatically. His head dropped, his shoulders slouched, and his feet shuffled as he faced the next batter. The poor pitcher never recovered psychologically and his body language told the story. The Lions admitted after the game that by the end of the first inning, they knew they had him! The Lions pitcher was in trouble off and on all night. He frequently faced batters with runners on base, but never gave in, and never gave up. He remained steady and stoic. If he was nervous or frightened, there was no evidence. His body language never said anything except calm and steady. The victory went to the Lions, physically, mentally, and with the winning score.

When you consider that research shows that body language accounts for 55% of every message you send, it's no wonder that other people sense what's really going on inside you, in spite of what you say. Everything, from fear to self-confidence, or humility to arrogance, is communicated through body language.

What is your body language saying?

The scary news for most people is that whatever they're thinking on a very private level is also what's being communicated by their body language, whether they intend it conveyed or not!

It's generally believed that body language doesn't lie.

The mood you choose to display when you arrive each morning to meet and greet your co-workers and customers is the first observable behavior noticed. Managers often underestimate the significance of these morning moments, but followers tend to take a "reading" from the leader's mood and internalize it. It's quite natural for people to make assumptions about the company's health and future based on the climate created by the mood of the leader. On any given day, the prospect of smooth sailing or impending doom is implied by the facial expressions of the leadership. The mood of the leader becomes the mood of the group as it ripples throughout an organization like electricity; the mood of the group never exceeds the mood of the leader.

For this reason, a leader must be a good actor, at least to the point of projecting hope and optimism. When sales are down or business is slow, it's appropriate to acknowledge those realities verbally. If you expect others to work with hope and optimism, as though the future is bright, you must display confidence when you walk through the door and announce that the numbers are slipping!

People are naturally drawn to energy. I'm not referring to the artificial hype that comes off as phony, or insincere. Genuine enthusiasm, which is rooted in a positive belief about the future, will attract others even when no words are being exchanged. The clues are caught in how you walk, the straightness of your back, the look on your face, and the twinkle in your eyes. Athletes look to their coaches, soldiers look to their generals, and children look to their parents — each one looking for a non-verbal signal that says, "Have faith, all is well."

Your assignment:

Here are some suggestions for using your body language in a productive way.

- Begin your day by thinking about the things that are going well in your life. Focus your attention on things for which you are appreciative. Mentally prepare yourself for the day's encounters by adopting an optimistic frame of mind.

- Smile – with your mouth and with your eyes! Your smile conveys warmth and energy, two things most people enjoy being around.

- Use eye contact to connect with others. Listen intently. Spend more time being interested, than interesting. Speak with people, not at them, using your facial expressions in a natural way to convey what you're feeling.

- Adopt the proud look. The U.S. Marines didn't pick this posture by accident. A straight back, shoulders square, head up, and chest out posture communicates confidence, strength, and security. There are other laid back postures that are very cool and appropriate in social settings, but in a business environment none of them gain credibility like the proud look. If you're not convinced, examine the world's best athletes to see how they carry themselves on the field of competition.

- Walk briskly, like you have someplace to go. Other people like to be in the company of those who have important places to go. It may seem symbolic to you now, but it's part of the entire energy package that attracts others.

Ask yourself what messages you'd like your body language to send about you. Design those messages with a purpose by paying attention to what your body is saying.

CHAPTER 19

USE THE THREE E'S

In his 1936 classic, *How to Win Friends and Influence People*, Dale Carnegie dedicates the entire first chapter to discussing three common mistakes in handling people. "Don't criticize, condemn, or complain." It seems to be human nature to engage in all three! It is tempting to criticize in order to feel superior. It is alluring to condemn in order to feel smart. It is enticing to complain in hopes that others will change. In reality, all three represent a recipe for how to lose friends and alienate people! I am convinced that...

> ...nothing will ruin a relationship faster, reduce trust to new lows, or cause more defensiveness than criticizing, condemning, or complaining.

Yet parents, coaches, teachers, and preachers repeatedly use these three strategies in an attempt to create change in human behavior. They don't work! The only consistent byproducts are defensiveness, resentment, alienation, and mistrust. Nothing good comes from the three C's.

However, there is an alternative. The three C's cannot be stopped by merely saying, "don't." They must be replaced by something superior and more constructive. They must be replaced by something that actually creates positive change in the people you care to influence, without destroying them along the way. The three E's have that kind of power:

Encourage – Give the gift of encouragement to help build self-confidence in others.

In its simplest form, encouragement means, "You can do it." The message is meant to inspire someone with courage or hope and fill them with strength of purpose. Encouragement can restore lost confidence and replace self-doubt. It accomplishes things within the human spirit that none of the three C's can provide – ever!

Dick Buttons, a commentator for Olympic figure skating events, told a story during a broadcast that I will never forget. He described a scene in which a young female skater, who was scheduled to compete, secluded herself in her hotel room due to a severe case of nerves. Her coach went to her room to provide the necessary encouragement. He said to her, "If you went to the most expensive restaurant in the city and ordered the most expensive meal on the menu, and you had no money in your pocket, you'd be a bit frightened, right?" The young girl nodded. "But if you went to the most expensive restaurant in the city and ordered the most expensive meal on the menu, and you had a hundred dollar bill in your pocket, would you be afraid?" The skater replied, "No, not at all!" "Right," said the coach, "and at this moment you have the hundred dollar bill in your pocket to pay for this performance. You've put in the work and learned your routine. You can do this."

There are times when you need to remind someone that they have the hundred dollar bill in their pocket. They can pay for their performance and need not sabotage themselves with self-doubt. You can be the one who recognizes the doubt, and reinstates self-confidence for someone who trusts your words. Don't miss your chance to be their wizard by saying, "You can do this."

Educate – Find creative ways to help others discover the answers they need.

It's been said that people are most dangerous when they don't know what they don't know! While that's probably true, you can't blame someone for not knowing that they don't know! However, you can help them discover the same lessons you've learned.

It's surprising how many athletic coaches, and middle management supervisors approach their instructional opportunities with criticism as their number one tool. These well-meaning "coaches" operate from the assumption that their job is to point out the flaws in other people's work. It is further assumed that if a flaw is pointed out, certainly the student will not make the same mistake again!

To illustrate this point in a workshop setting, I have frequently given each of five volunteers a broom. The instructions consist of a single sentence. "Please balance the broom vertically for one minute, using only your index finger, with the bristles pointed toward the ceiling." Usually three or four participants will struggle with this assignment as they chase the misbehaving broom around the front of the room. Of course, it's my job at this point to say critical things like, "That's not the way to do it!" "C'mon, get it right!" "I told you to balance the broom for a minute." "Work harder and figure it out!" "You're not very good at this." Naturally, this just adds to the embarrassment of my students and creates the distraction of more self-doubt, and less success.

As is true in every new skill, there's a trick to the trick, and broom balancing is no exception. To create success for each of my volunteers it's necessary to create a different environment, and provide the important exposure to the information they are missing. At this point, I reassure everyone in the group that within just a few short minutes they will be successful. Next, I identify the one or two people who have been successful and ask them to demonstrate. Interestingly, sometimes they are successful but don't know why they are! Eventually the entire group discovers the secret to broom balancing: Keep your eyes focused on the top of the broom at all times. On the next attempt everyone makes significant progress or meets the one-minute goal. The turning point for each person was discovering new information. This is the essence of education.

When you educate others by exposing them to new concepts in a non-threatening way, you help them raise their game. Higher self-esteem and increased self-confidence replace the fear of failure and self-doubt. Ask any Little League baseball player if he thinks the coach yelling at him improves his base-running skills. He may appear to run faster, but he doesn't know how to run the bases any better until he is taught! Adults in the workplace are just bigger Little Leaguers; the issues are the same. Scolding or embarrassing poor performers builds walls of mistrust and hinders improvement. When you take the time to educate those who are struggling by sharing the little "tricks to the trick," you will be valued as a people-builder.

Edify – Build up other people with your words.

To edify someone means to build him or her up. Most often, this is done by saying positive and complimentary things about them, whether they are present or not. Just as negative gossip can destroy someone's image, edifying has the power to raise someone's stock in the eyes of others.

Picture you standing in front of someone and holding a mirror for them to see their own reflection. When you edify someone, you are basically accomplishing the same thing. As you describe the person you see in them, they receive a picture of specific qualities or potential that increases their self-esteem. You help them see attributes they may not have appreciated about themselves.

The more specific the observations, the more helpful they are. A comment like, "Oh, I think you're just great" has very little value because "great" is generic and non-specific. But if you told someone, "I'm so impressed with your attention to detail for all our projects" – that's edifying! When you comment to others, "Bill is handling the negative feedback from our harshest critics like a real pro…he's so patient with them." Bill's perceived value goes up and so does his credibility. This helps Bill and it helps the team, as long as these comments are sincere and truthful. Others see insincere comments or obviously inaccurate statements as manipulative or phony.

As you learn to edify others with authentic and honest comments, your own credibility will be enhanced. Lifting up the qualities of others creates a positive and healthy environment for everyone involved. Edifying becomes the accepted norm. Tearing others down quickly seems out of place and unthinkable. Build your reputation as one who increases the value people see in each other.

> *"Change the way you look at things, and*
> *the things you look at change."*
> *— Wayne Dwyer, author*

Your assignment:
Your goal is to use each of the three E's at least once every day. To help yourself monitor your progress, place three quarters in a pocket on your left side each morning. Each time you encourage, educate, or edify someone during the day, move one of the quarters from a left-hand pocket to a right-hand pocket. By the end of the day all the quarters should be transferred. As you improve your skills, increase the number of quarters!

CHAPTER 20

SOCRATES HAD IT RIGHT

As I sat in a busy airport one night, I saw a little toddler running down the concourse next to his dad. Suddenly, the little guy caught his toe and ended up with a face-plant and a dead stop on the hard floor. His dad quickly turned around as the boy picked himself up off the floor and with concern asked, "What did you hit?", referring to knee, elbow, or chin. The boy looked up at his dad in utter disbelief and pointed at the floor. I guess the answer seemed obvious to the boy, but perhaps the question wasn't as clear as it appeared to the dad!

Asking good questions may be one of the most significant skills to learn. Somewhere in the development of most adults a strange thing happens at almost exactly the same moment as the arrival of a diploma or a promotion. A mental switch gets thrown and what was an intelligent question-asking human being (since early childhood) becomes an answer-telling machine – all-knowing, all seeing, and certain of everything! It's as if any hesitation or inquiry indicates incompetence. Every situation in the workplace or home life presents you with two options: 1) Jump to a conclusion, or 2) Ask a question to learn more. Credibility goes to those who ask probing questions, listen, and then decide.

Socrates taught his students by asking, not telling. He posed a series of questions to help people determine their underlying beliefs. He wanted to know about their assumptions and their current level of understanding. By asking really good questions, Socrates stimulated his students to think and make intellectual discoveries. Socrates once said, "I know you won't believe me, but the highest form of human excellence is to question oneself and others."

It's tempting to slip into "tell mode" and find some kind of satisfaction in being the answer man. It might create a sense of self-importance to know the answers to lots of questions. It will also appear that lots of people depend on you, perhaps to the point where they stop thinking for themselves. But those who answer questions don't learn as much or grow as deeply as those who ask questions.

The challenge here, however, is not just remembering to ask questions, but to ask effective questions – really good questions – the kind that take you somewhere. There are all kinds of Bozo questions. A Bozo question is the kind that narrows the scope of a conversation rather than widening it. This usually happens because of one or more of the following characteristics.

- It is based on negative assumptions
- It contains accusations or insinuations of wrongdoing
- It creates or invites defensiveness
- It has a sarcastic tone

Here are some examples of Bozo questions:

Why did you do it?

Don't you know any better?

Why are you behind schedule?

What's your problem?

Who do you think you are?

Are you trying to make this difficult?

Why are you so far behind?

Who isn't doing it right?

Who blew it?

Who made that decision?

Effective questions are open-ended and cannot be answered with a yes or no. They are an honest inquiry that is designed to make it safe for the person being asked to think and to discover by way of:

- sharing their thoughts
- sharing their feelings
- sharing their opinions
- sharing their ideas
- sharing their concerns

Effective questions also make it possible for the person asking the question to learn more about the subject than what they actually asked for!

In a safe environment, those being asked a thought-provoking question will search for meaningful answers and will think and speak spontaneously.

Here are some examples of great questions that will provide an open and honest dialogue:

How do you feel about this assignment?

What's working the best so far?

If you have any concerns, what would they be at this point?

What's your vision of the outcome?

What's your number one goal?

What key events need to happen for you to reach our goal?

How will this benefit our customers?

What's the primary cause of your success so far?

If you had it to do over again, what would you do differently?

What else can you share with me now?

In what way can I help you?

What lessons have you learned?

The boy on first base was an experienced base runner for a thirteen-year old. Kevin had played baseball since he was five. But, when the batter hit a line drive to right field, Kevin found himself too far away from first base when the right fielder made a great catch, and he couldn't get back in time to avoid the double play. The first base coach went ballistic, beginning with a Bozo question. "What's wrong with you?" He then went on to yell about Kevin's costly mistake and poor judgment. Kevin tried to explain, but couldn't get a word in. When he returned to the dugout he received a second reprimand from the assistant coach, which just happened to be his own dad. In wasn't until all the accusations ended that Kevin finally got to say the one thing that really mattered. It wasn't until the two coaches had unloaded their emotions on the boy that he could provide an answer to the question no one had bothered to ask. Why was he so far off first base? "Dad, the third base coach gave me the steal sign before the pitch was thrown." No one had bothered to ask the one intelligent question that would have provided the answer.

<u>Your assignment:</u>

Find three opportunities today to do the following:

1. Observe a situation, or listen to someone's description of a situation.

2. Suspend any judgment or mental critique.

3. Ask a really good open-ended question that will generate thinking and discovery.

CHAPTER 21

GIVE THE GIFT OF SILENCE

I was waiting in the parking lot at the usual time. As the basketball players came out of the gym I noticed my ten-year-old's head was hanging low. When he got in the car, and slammed the door, I asked, "How was practice?" "I hate my coach" was the reply. This kind of response did not sit well with me. Three thoughts rushed to my brain, all fighting for priority to be delivered with a correcting tone. First, I thought, "I've taught you not to speak so disrespectfully about any coach or adult." Secondly, I thought, "Are you kidding? This guy is a great coach – one of the best!" And thirdly, "Do you have any idea how hard I worked to make sure you were placed on this guy's team?" For some odd reason I chose not to say any of those condemning thoughts, and instead only three words came out of my mouth. Perhaps they are the three best words I've ever accidentally said. "Tell me more."

My son went on to explain some things that happened during practice. I knew I wasn't getting the whole story yet, so I added, "What else happened?" Eventually – and it took a little while – we got to the part where he admitted to getting side-tracked during practice, got caught goofing off during one of the drills, and was reprimanded. In the final analysis, my son was embarrassed by the coach's reprimand in front of the other boys and that is what really led to the declaration, "I hate my coach."

The point of this story is that my first, second, and third thoughts, if delivered immediately, would have missed the mark by a mile. They were totally irrelevant in view of the facts, which would never have been revealed if I'd blurted out my little speech.

I had been guilty more than once of jumping the gun with a quick response, but I learned so much more this time with just three little words – "tell me more."

The complete story gave me much more insight into my son and how he thinks and reacts.

Listening is an art and a skill. It requires discipline and focused attention. When you give the gift of silence you allow others the chance to think and process their thoughts. The time required to do this varies tremendously. Some people think their thoughts out loud where everyone can hear them, and then they do the editing in public, too: "Here's what I really mean." They might revise their initial version several times. Others process everything internally, preferring not to share the end result until it is edited and refined to a finished product.

These people never share a verbal "rough draft."

Listening to the first of these two groups is easy because they don't make you wait very long. However, the second group requires patience by those who eagerly await an explanation or a report about what's going on. Impatience at this point will cause you to jump straight into "tell mode," as in, "Let me tell you what I think." The lecture that follows is usually not appreciated or helpful.

To gain credibility, learn to give space and time to others before making your verbal contribution. Give the gift of silence while people consider their actions and their words. Use phrases like "Tell me more" and "What else?" to prompt more information that will give you a fuller understanding of people and situations. Not only will this build trust, but it will also keep you from making incorrect assumptions about people and events.

Your assignment:

Find an opportunity at home, at work, and in a social setting to use the phrase, "Tell me more." Resist the temptation to respond to people in these three settings with your own opinions or thoughts until after at least two attempts at giving the gift of silence so they can tell you more of what's on their mind.

SECTION FOUR

HAVE SOMETHING NEW: MAKE THE SIX CRUCIAL TURNS OF CHUMP TO CHAMP LEADERSHIP

The purpose of this section is to help you envision the potential outcome of your journey. What kind of results could you expect from becoming something new (Section Two), and doing something new (Section Three)? There's got to be a payoff from increasing your personal credibility. If to be transformed allows you to do distinguishing things, what will you have? As a person of high credibility, you will experience higher levels of success and satisfaction in six specific areas of your life. Each of the six represents leadership's most crucial situations for work and home. This is where champs shine and chumps whine.

1. Have mature conversations that build strong healthy relationships.
2. Have high levels of trust from others.

3. Have constructive and productive conflict.

4. Have those you influence generate their own motivation from within.

5. Have those you influence enjoy significant results from your coaching.

6. Have those you influence make strong commitments to necessary change.

Each of these six will be affected by one powerful force that weaves its way through all your opportunities in each of life's arenas – emotional intelligence – and that is where Section Four begins.

One of the most beautiful events in water skiing is the slalom event. It is also one of the most demanding. The towboat travels straight down the center of the slalom course at a constant speed while the skier cuts back and forth, carving six turns, using the pull of the boat for speed and direction. The boat is an ever-present force at every turn.

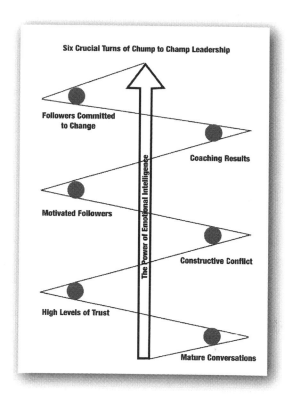

Six Crucial Turns of Chump to Champ Leadership

In much the same way, as you discover your leadership potential and the benefits of your increased credibility, your efficiency and effectiveness will come from a force felt at every turn. As you face the six opportunities listed above, your emotional maturity (EQ – Emotional Quotient) can be the ever-present supplier of power, or it can be your Achilles' heel. It's up to you to use it wisely.

CHAPTER 22

THE POWER OF EMOTIONS

One of the most powerful tools in your leadership toolbox is the power of emotions, and the most significant question is whether you control them, or they control you!

If you think back to your high school days, who was it that appeared to be headed for success? The kids with the highest grades and the best test scores. Right? From an early age you and I were convinced that the kids with the highest IQ were destined to be the most successful adults. Now that you are an adult, has it turned out that only the kids with great scores have become successful? In fact, did great grades and high test scores always produce successful careers? You probably know the answer to that one. Absolutely not!

So, obviously there's something else going on besides IQ when it comes to succeeding in business and succeeding in life. There's another game being played that some people don't even know about! The name of the game is EQ – Emotional Quotient. In *How to Win Friends & Influence People*,

Dale Carnegie made this statement: "About 15% of one's financial success is due to one's technical knowledge and about 85% is due to skill in human engineering – to personality and the ability to lead people." The term EQ had not been created in 1936, but the concept of "emotional maturity" was clearly on Carnegie's mind.

I'm not talking about whether you are emotional or not. I'm not talking about whether you show your emotions or keep them hidden. I am talking about being honest about your emotions, and being smart with them. I am talking about the power of emotions and how those emotions can be used in a positive way to create productive relationships. The extreme flip side is when emotions take control producing disastrous results. Obviously, both IQ and EQ are important, but very different.

Think of it this way. Our Intelligence Quotient (IQ) is connected to our head and our thinking, and our Emotional Quotient (EQ) is connected to our heart and our feelings. Logically, you know it's not a good idea to scream at someone or take a swing at them; however, you may feel the impulse to do exactly that! In fact, many people become emotionally hijacked, which means they lose control to their emotions. It's your emotional intelligence that helps you overcome those impulses and gives you self-control over your emotions at that critical moment. Today's research indicates that your emotional intelligence level is a better indicator of your success in life than your intellectual intelligence.

Your EQ is more significant than your IQ. This is great news! Why? Because, unlike your IQ, your EQ can be improved!

Starting today, you can take steps to increase your emotional intelligence to the point where your relationships will be better, your leadership more effective, and your followers are more productive.

Let's identify the primary emotions you might encounter in the average day, but divide them into two categories. Grab a piece of paper and draw a line down the middle. At the top of one column write "Unproductive Emotions" and on the other side write "Productive Emotions."

Some emotions are unproductive or even destructive in the workplace. Which ones did you list? Here are some examples: resentment, anger, hostility, gloom, self-pity, dread, fear, contempt, guilt, humiliation, and shame – none of these are positive or productive.

On the other hand, which emotions should we encourage and hope to see in each other?

Here are a few: happiness, joy, contentment, relief, delight, pride, gratification, satisfaction, acceptance, trust, friendliness, kindness, devotion, optimism, and hopefulness are all examples of positive and productive emotions.

As a leader, your job is to create an environment where the more productive emotions show up the majority of the time and the unproductive emotions are rarer. Please remember, people are entitled to feel whatever emotion they experience, because we can't always control what we feel. We can control how we act, and leaders have a responsibility to generate positive emotions by their words and actions every day.

Research by the Gallup Organization demonstrated that when positive emotions are generated in the workplace at a ratio of five to one over negative emotions, people are more productive, more engaged with co-workers, receive higher satisfaction from customers, and have better safety records. An excellent resource for more information is Tom Rath and Don Clifton's book, *How Full is Your Bucket*.

When leaders know how to use the power of emotions, some of the most important activities of the day are affected in a positive way. Let's take a look at a few of these scenarios, each one handled in two different ways. In each case, you'll find a question or a statement followed by two responses. The first response is a low EQ response and the second reflects a higher EQ response. What differences do you notice between them?

Decision Making:

"Have you made a decision yet regarding my vacation request?"

Responses:

1. "I'm in a lousy mood today, so the answer to your question is No!"
2. "I'm not thinking very clearly right now so let me think about this decision for a little longer before I respond."

The second response indicates self-awareness of an emotional condition that might affect decision making.

Providing Coaching & Feedback:

"I'm really struggling with the new program – it's hard."

Responses:

1. "We don't have all week for you to learn this. C'mon, get going and try it again."
2. "I believe in you and I think you'll be more comfortable with this new skill by Wednesday afternoon. However, if you need more time or more coaching let me know by Wednesday morning."

The second response demonstrates patience and encouragement in spite of the urgency of the situation.

Waiting For Information:

"I don't have that report ready quite yet."

Responses:

1. "I asked for this in plenty of time. What's your problem?"
2. "I know I can be impatient at times. Tell me what obstacles you're running into so I understand."

Self-control and a willingness to understand can be heard in the second response.

Handling A Conflict:

"I don't necessarily agree with this method."

Responses:

1. "This is the way it should be. I know what I'm doing."
2. "I know we both have strong feelings about this issue. Please explain your position so I can think about it." Understanding the feelings of others (social awareness) and relationship management is demonstrated in the second response.

Listening To An Employee's Issue:

"I'm sick and tired of getting the run-around from them."

Responses:

1. "I don't want to hear whining about that again."
2. "I understand this is frustrating for you. What solutions can you suggest?"

The second response shows empathy and an effort to build upon the existing relationship.

In each case above, the first response is a reaction without much thought. It comes from an impulse to the brain and the words follow quickly. In the second response, the speaker is more self-aware of the emotions being experienced and is, therefore, more thoughtful before speaking.

Have you heard that some athletes have fast-twitch muscles? These muscles are quick responders and very explosive. In a similar way, we are vulnerable to a kind of fast-twitch emotion – and we call them "impulses." They are feelings we have a split second ahead of any thoughts. When someone insults you or criticizes your work, the initial feeling you have of hurt or anger is a fast-twitch emotion that you feel instantly without thinking. Now, here's the question: "Do you know yourself well enough to recognize the feeling you're having, or do you get caught up in it so much that you can only resent the injustice of it all?

Here's an old Japanese story from Daniel Goleman's book, *Emotional Intelligence.* A samurai swordsman challenged a wise Zen master to explain the difference between heaven and hell. The monk rebuked the samurai by saying he had no time to waste on such an ordinary man. With his honor insulted, the samurai pulled out his sword and angrily threatened the monk, reminding him that he could kill him in an instant for his disrespect. At that point the Zen master calmly replied, "That, sir, is hell." The samurai was suddenly aware of the lesson and the anger that had a hold on him. He bowed politely and thanked the master for this insight, at which point, the wise Zen master replied,

"And that, sir, is heaven."

Understanding yourself is knowing the difference between being controlled by a feeling, and being aware that you're being controlled by a feeling!

This higher degree of self-awareness means you are aware of your moods at the very moment you're having them. You understand your own moods and the effect they have on you.

Without this understanding of self, you can become a victim of a fast-twitch reaction, and sometimes with terrible consequences. In 1999, a young Orlando, Florida mother hit her eight-year-old daughter with a baseball bat for wetting her pants. Afterwards, she wondered out loud, "What have I done?" We call this being emotionally hijacked – being controlled by an impulse and unaware of the control it has until after a regrettable behavior.

Okay, it's time for you to take a look at your emotional experiences. This exercise is designed to help you become more self-aware; in other words, to understand yourself in particular situations.

Write down the following list of emotions on a piece of paper.

1. Anger
2. Sadness
3. Fear
4. Disgust
5. Shame
6. Jealousy

After each word, describe a specific situation when you experienced that emotion and where it came from. Then ask yourself:

1. What are the recognizable signs that I'm in the grip of this particular emotion?
2. How can I sense and identify that particular emotion within me?
3. What must I do so I can remain in control of my actions in spite of the emotion I'm feeling?

Improving your personal EQ is a "do-it-to-myself" project and begins with knowing the answers to these questions. As you encounter and respond to each of the Six Crucial Turns of Leadership described on the following pages, you will carve your reputation and have the results you deserve.

"I don't let my mouth say nothin' my head can't stand."
— *Louis Armstrong, entertainer*

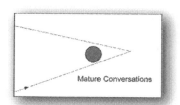

Mature Conversations

CHAPTER 23

TURN #1 - HAVE MATURE CONVERSATIONS AND HEALTHY RELATIONSHIPS

"**Y**ou wouldn't believe how Rebecca talks to her mother. She's very disrespectful and sarcastic, and her mom just takes it without saying a word." This is the report we received from our daughter at a young age after visiting a school friend's home. This was a revelation of sorts for our daughter who was twelve at the time. She couldn't understand the whole scene because in her mind neither her friend nor the friend's mother was playing her part the way she should.

It's been said that nothing is more indicative of the health of a relationship than the kind of conversations that happen within it. Healthy, thriving, respectful relationships have constructive, productive, respectful conversations – and usually about worthwhile topics. Troubled, deteriorating, poisonous relationships are saturated with sarcastic, condescending, disrespectful conversations – and frequently focus on petty or small topics.

If you're wondering how we got this way, just turn on your television and listen to the content and the tone of the conversations in most of today's sitcoms. If the average American is watching six to seven hours of television a day, as many studies suggest, the exposure to shallow, self-serving dialogue is overwhelming. No wonder children grow up confused about how to resolve conflict, how to express empathy, or how to deliver a sincere apology. If television is shaping their conversational skills, there's a big problem!

When it comes to conversational skills, a caveman mentality shows up quite frequently. Nature's response to a threat is fight or flight— to engage in combat or run the other way.

Unfortunately, those same two choices show up as the primary responses for people who do not know how to have healthy conversations. The degree of "fight" can range anywhere from giving a lecture to an all out verbal attack. When people choose the "flight" response, they typically shut down, grow silent, and withhold any meaningful contribution to the conversation. Neither of these extremes can be called healthy, and too much of either one will destroy relationships quickly.

Here's the question. What kind of conversations would you like to have with the people in your life? How would you like your conversations to sound and feel? Imagine the kind of exchanges you'd expect from a champ – someone who is mature, secure, and supportive of others, yet firm in his convictions about right and wrong. Here are some suggestions about the kind of conversations a champ can have.

Respectfulness

When conversation is at its best, three key elements are present, over and above listening. I don't mean to minimize listening. It is crucial to having a healthy conversation because it indicates that you are truly interested in what's being said to you. Listening is just one of the signs of respect. I prefer to list respectfulness as the first element of a healthy conversation, and there are many ways to show it. As a champ, it is your nature to demonstrate a reverence for the person to whom you speak. Because of who you are, you naturally speak in a tone, project a body language, and listen in a way that says you respect them. It is an atmosphere you choose to bring to every conversation. It comes across in your tone of voice, facial expressions, and body language. It means you are conscientious about your entire presentation. This climate represents an underlying belief in the value of people and their conversational content. During every conversation where respectfulness is projected, invisible emotional deposits are being made in the subconscious mind of those with whom you speak. For this reason, the relationship is enhanced.

Empathy

Healthy conversations are enjoyed by people who are aware and sensitive to the needs of others. As a champ, you know that people have emotional needs, often different from your own at any given time. It's not your job to take care of everyone's needs, but because you are an encourager and a people-builder you seek to understand other people's fears, pride, frustration, anxiety, and expectations. Understanding these emotional forces during conversations allows you to demonstrate patience and avoid judgment. The art of empathy is available only to those who know themselves so well that they recognize someone's emotional state as familiar to their own experience. This familiarity makes it possible for you to express an understanding of the feelings you sense in others. A champ can help a conversation get past the emotional content by delivering a meaningful empathy statement at just the right moment. When you say, "I understand this is frustrating for you" or "I know this is not what you expected to happen," the conversation can move forward to the factual content. Always address the emotional content of a conversation ahead of factual content.

The Search For Truth

Another element of a healthy conversation is the free, unencumbered flow of information (feelings, facts, opinions, impressions). This exchange, at its best, is a learning experience for everyone involved. Champs understand the enormous potential of a healthy conversation, and they are eager for the full and complete disclosure of all available data to come freely from all participants. Your vision of a great conversation is everyone going away more knowledgeable and wiser for having been part of the exchange. If all participants are enriched by the experience and if all have grown in some way, perhaps the truth was nearby. This kind of conversation is only possible if all participants are both free and encouraged to bring all that they have to the discussion. Champs create the atmosphere for that to happen because they are truth seekers by nature. They are not afraid of what might be discovered.

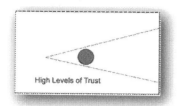
High Levels of Trust

CHAPTER 24

TURN #2 - HAVE HIGH LEVELS OF TRUST FROM YOUR FOLLOWERS

As you can see from reading the preceding chapter, your success at having mature, healthy conversations is a crucial turning point in earning high levels of trust from others. Everyone talks about the importance of trust, but it's surprising how few people understand what it is and how it works. Entire books are dedicated to this one critical component of human interaction. In its simplest form, trust is acting on a belief. When you believe someone will take some action on your behalf, like watching your children while you are away, or looking after your most important client while you are on vacation, you feel free to turn over the responsibility. Internally, you have asked yourself questions like, "Can I trust them to pay attention? Can I trust their skills? Can I trust their understanding of how important it is to care for these people?" Your trust in them is applied when you actually leave the task to them. Until you leave, it's only a belief on your part, but not actual trust. Trust is demonstrated with action. It's a contradiction when you say, "I trust you, but I'm not leaving this to you."

One of the big payoffs of your chump to champ journey will be high levels of trust from others. As they see your champ-like behaviors (from Section Two) others will see and believe that you not only mean them no harm, but you are their advocate. You want what is best for them, and you are willing to give time and energy to help them achieve their goals. In a very similar way, the trainers of animals, like the killer whales at Sea World of Orlando, spend months and years building a bond of trust that reassures the animals that the trainers mean no harm. This is also the basis of the Hippocratic Oath taken by the medical profession: "Do no harm." Of course, you want a doctor you can trust – one who is committed and skilled to help you, and at the very least, do you no harm!

The amount of trust people have within any organization – your family life or your work life – reveals itself in everyday actions. Here is a sample of the kind of trusting actions you can expect from those who trust, as compared to those who do not trust.

Low-Trust Behaviors	High-Trust Behaviors
Guarded conversatios, being careful with one's words.	Open and honest dialogue, feeling free to tell the truth.
Controlling situations and decisions, keeping a close guard on who has power.	Sharing information and decision making responsibilities, sharing power.
Pushing for win/lose solutions to conflict.	Pushing for win/win solutions to conflict.
Primary pronouns used - "us" and "them."	Primary pronouns used - "we."
Blaming and finger pointing when things go wrong.	Open assessment of what went wrong without much concern about who did what.
Disloyalty to the the team when under pressure.	Loyalty to the team when under pressure.
Protecting self and promoting self.	Protecting others and promoting others
Confidentiality not respected, gossip issues.	Confidentiality respected, gossip avoided.

As someone who has transformed himself or herself to a new level of personal performance (champ), and who is doing beneficial things for others, you will notice more trusting behaviors by those around you. The environment you have created lends itself to higher levels of trust, because you show your trust in others first.

When this is not the case, a lack of trust usually manifests itself in consistent ways. People who feel fearful in any environment tend to protect themselves. They avoid offering ideas, avoid solving problems on their own, and avoid taking the initiative, because it's too risky. They have a fear of being taken advantage of, fear of failure, fear of being criticized, or a fear of being hurt emotionally by having weaknesses exposed. Ultimately, the worst fear is the fear of being rejected or abandoned. You might also see behaviors designed to promote oneself. Bragging, boasting, and calling attention to personal achievements is a response to pride, but also denotes a lack of trust in relationships. This kind of environment becomes toxic because the people in it do not feel safe.

But you are a champ, so you know that exposing your own vulnerability is a trust-building characteristic. If others notice that you feel safe sharing your weaknesses and admitting your frailties, it signals that you trust them with your reputation. Giving away trust earns more trust.

Managers and supervisors often get caught up in a game of "looking good," or faking certainty when they don't know the answers. This is reminiscent of parents who might not know why they've just given a command to their children, but they feel comfortable with, "because I said so" as the ultimate way to save face! The irony in all this is that your followers at work – just like your children at home – know that you're not being authentic. All your attempts to create the illusion of being in total control detract from whatever credibility you had in the first place.

Credibility is the key ingredient in leadership. The Latin root word is "credo," which means, "I believe" or "I trust."

Credibility, like credit from a bank, is given to those who are trusted or believed. Therefore, credibility is extended to the leaders or parents, whom they find...believable! If you're not believable, or not trusted to represent yourself honestly, you will have little credibility with anyone. It may be the biggest paradox in organizations today; knowledge is honored, while pretending to know it all is disdained.

It takes courage to be authentic with peers and followers, but the end result is stronger relationships built on trust. Gone is the illusion of perfection, which everyone knows doesn't exist anyway. In its place is the image of someone who is aware of the true human condition – flawed and vulnerable, but ready to learn lessons and move on. This is the kind of leader who can be trusted to lift others to opportunities of leadership as well.

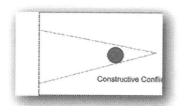

Constructive Conflict

CHAPTER 25

TURN #3 - HAVE CONSTRUCTIVE CONFLICT

One of the greatest misconceptions is that conflict is bad, and should be avoided at all costs. For this reason, many people run from almost every conflict situation and rarely get to experience productive or constructive conflict. Conflict is neither good nor bad. It's just a reality of life that can be handled constructively or destructively. Some skills are required to make it constructive, and you've learned many of them on your journey from chump to champ.

One definition of conflict is that it is the tension created when people have concerns that appear to be threatened by the concerns of others. These concerns can be things like personal pride, ego, and authority, or obvious possessions like money, oil, and property. In a conflict, people choose a position and pursue an outcome that meets their needs. The energy put into the conflict depends upon its importance to those involved. If you don't care about being right regarding your prediction of today's weather, you probably won't engage in a conflict over it. However, if you are the weatherman for a local news station, your pride may entice you to defend your prediction vehemently to anyone who challenges it.

Conflict comes in a variety of flavors: man vs. nature, man vs. technology, man vs. himself, and man vs. man. It's the last one that seems to be most complex and the hardest to get right. We witness this kind of conflict frequently. In fact, we actually go looking for it when we want entertainment. Every movie you've ever seen, every book you've ever read, and every television show you've ever watched was created around one important question – "What is the conflict within this story?"

You watch a story develop to see how the conflict unfolds, and how the conflict is resolved. You want the conflict to be resolved. A movie that ends without resolving the main conflict is disappointing. You might even feel let down by such an ending. In the same way, we feel better about the conflicts in our lives when they are resolved. Unresolved conflict feels frustrating, disappointing, and unfinished. Conflicts that are resolved in a manner that damages or destroys relationships are not satisfying either.

The question is, "How can we engage in conflict in a manner that meets our respective needs, produces creative solutions, and at the same time enhances relationships?" Is it possible?

Imagine you are in a room and seated around a large conference table with eleven other people. It is a diverse group with various ages, educational backgrounds, and demographics represented. There is an issue to be resolved and many conflicting concerns are represented in the room. As various individuals begin to speak, offering their ideas and strategies, you notice each idea presented takes the shape of a small balloon rising above the head of its author. The balloon hovers there for all to see. No one's name is on the balloon, because it is actually an idea and ideas belong to everyone. As more ideas (balloons) begin to float around the room, the participants can compare them, weigh their strengths and feasibilities, and make appreciative comments about their preferences. They might speak passionately about elements that are important to them. Given enough time, and assuming the entire group is determined to arrive at the "best" answer, this collaborative scenario can play out successfully. The final answer could be something so creative and imaginative that none of the members saw it before arriving in the room. The solution would be declared a win/win for everyone. When conflict is handled this way, new creative answers are discovered, old problems are solved, trust is enhanced, and relationships are improved...thanks to a constructive approach to the conflict.

However, this very same scene can also play out very differently. The collaborative atmosphere of the participants could instead become a competitive, self-serving, idea-attacking, verbal brawl. One single factor causes this change – idea ownership. Once individuals take personal ownership of ideas and attach themselves personally to those ideas, they tend to fight for them based on personal pride and personal ego. When a member of the group shows disapproval of an idea by words and tone of voice, it gets personal. Idea ownership ("Hey, that's my idea!") leads the author of an idea to see objections as a negative personal commentary.

Once things get personal, the stage is set for a competitive struggle for a win/lose finish. There will be a resolution, but there will also be two other unfortunate byproducts: hurt feelings and damaged relationships. In addition, the answer may not represent the group's "best." I once heard a man say that he'd like to learn how to win all arguments with his friends. I told him that it was possible to learn to do this, but soon there would be something he would not have – friends! Generally speaking, cooper*ativeness* in a conflict is always directly related to how much concern the participants have for their relationship with each other.

Highly effective people (champs) understand this concept and are willing to work with the ambiguity of group dynamics. They are willing to risk not knowing the answer in advance, and possibly not getting the answer they had hoped for. They trust the process and the other champs in the room. The other members in the conflict are seen as conflict partners, not conflict enemies. While this is time consuming and not used for quick decisions – like which door to use when the building is on fire – it is the best way to arrive at creative solutions to complex issues and enhance relationships at the same time.

A room full of people who are not aware of how collaboration works (chumps) will argue blindly, and quite possibly resort to name calling and personal attacks over emotionally charged issues.

Their goal is to get their way, regardless of the cost to relationships. The problem is, pigs don't know that pigs stink!

This can be quite frustrating for any champs in the room.

However, there is one kind of conflict when even champs must take a non-collaborative position. When a conflict emerges that threatens established core values, or calls for abandoning/violating such values, there's no room for a compromise. Can you imagine a safety director on a construction site telling his crew, "Look, I know you don't like wearing the safety glasses, so will you at least wear them on one eye?" "I know the hard hats are uncomfortable, so will you just wear them half the time?" Or, how about this one: "If you're going to steal from the company, could you just steal a little bit, but not a lot?"

These issues call for a win/lose resolution when people press for a compromise on core values. When it comes to ethics in medicine, safety at a construction site, cleanliness in a restaurant, or confidentiality in a human resources office – the 50% solution is not acceptable. Every organization and every family must declare its non-negotiables. All those who accept membership in an organization, from employees in a company to children in a family, will be looking to the champs for the example of how to deal with the corresponding conflicts.

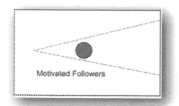

Motivated Followers

CHAPTER 26

TURN #4 - HAVE MOTIVATED FOLLOWERS

As you journey from chump to champ, your increased credibility will increase your influence over others. Regardless of the formal role you play in various organizations, you will find yourself influencing the thinking and actions of an increasing number of people. By definition, you will be seen as a leader whether you have a title or not. After all, leadership is the degree of influence you have with others. Those who influence only a few are still exerting leadership. Those who influence thousands or hundreds of thousands are exerting significant amounts of leadership. The point of this is that all leaders want to have motivated followers. That's how things get done. Consequently, many leaders believe it is their responsibility to motivate the followers, and many followers agree.

It always bothers me when I'm introduced as a "motivational" speaker. The use of that term automatically suggests that at the end of my presentation the members of the audience should be more motivated than they were at the beginning of my speech. Therefore, my value as a speaker hinges on whether or not the members of my audience go out into their world and do something that they otherwise wouldn't have done. If they do, I'm a success, and if they don't, I'm a dud! Wow, that feels like a huge responsibility for a speaker to carry. Does that responsibility really rest with a speaker, a leader, a manager, a coach, a teacher, or a preacher? Or, does that responsibility rest with those who hear the message of the speaker, the leader, the manager, the coach, the teacher, or the preacher? Herein lays the mystery of motivation and it raises the fundamental question:

Can you motivate another person? The short answer is – believe it or not – no.

Anything – a great book, a great speaker, or a great movie – can *inspire* someone. Inspiration is not the same as motivation. How many times have you felt inspired, and then done absolutely nothing? You can be inspired (a feeling) by someone's story about their tremendous weight loss, and then say "Please pass the French fries." Yes, you are inspired, but not motivated. Only when you deny yourself the French fries can we say you are motivated.

All motivation comes from within each and every one of us. It's an inside job! You can't make anyone do anything! Ask Gandhi. Ask Martin Luther King. Ask Abraham Lincoln. Ask any great leader, or any parent. People choose to follow leaders. They choose to take action. When you use threats of pain or punishment to create action in others, the person who responds to avoid those consequences is not motivated – they are merely complying. The only one truly motivated is the one delivering the threat! Do not mistake compliance with motivation.

Here's a simple definition from Frederick Hertzberg that will make sense of this. "Motivation is the pursuit of an unmet need."

The word pursuit makes it clear that there is action that comes from a motive – an unmet need.

If you decide to lose weight and take the action of going to the gym or changing your diet, it's because you have an unmet need to weigh less, or you want to look differently than you do now. The motivation for the work comes from within. It is a choice.

So, how do you as a champ have those you influence generate their own motivation from within? How do you have motivated followers? You'll discover the answer by playing an imaginary game called "What if you couldn't pay them?"

Imagine that suddenly there was no money to pay anyone for his or her time or efforts. Imagine that you had to rely totally on volunteers to get the *exact same* amount of work accomplished as when there were wages. What strategies would you use to attract volunteers? If you've ever been part of a volunteer organization this exercise will be a little easier for you. Ask yourself, why do volunteers work so hard, so generously, and with such a high level of commitment when they're not getting paid? The number one answer is that they believe in the cause! When people believe in a cause and share a vision, they often find that some of their personal unmet needs are met by being part of that worthwhile cause.

Here are the ten most important steps for attracting motivated people, and the corresponding needs followers are pursuing in the workplace.

Strategy to Attract Motivated People	The Unmet Need That Must Be Pursued
Share the vision of where you're going, what the end result will look like, and who will benefit	A worthwhile cause to believe in.
Discover their passion, their skills, and what activities give them feelings of fulfillment.	A task that is enjoyable.
Convey how their contribution is important and worthwhile.	A task that is significant and impactful.
Provide training and feedback.	Personal growth and development.
Work with them (lead by example).	Camaraderie and something to aspire to.
Show appreciation.	To feel appreciated and valuable.
Ask for their input.	To feel credible.
Ask for their feedback.	To feel important.
Recognize their accomplishments.	To receive praise and be admired.
Celebrate their accomplishments.	To experience fellowship over milestones and victory.

You've heard the old saying, "You can lead a horse to water, but you can't make him drink." Many people – parents and leaders alike – keep wondering, "How can I get my horse to drink?" As Hertzberg said, a better question is, "What makes my horse thirsty?" If you know the unmet needs of your people, then it becomes a matter of providing the opportunities for those people to pursue the meeting of those needs. If you've provided the right opportunity, they will demonstrate their motivation.

Champs have motivated followers, because champs are excellent at discovering unmet needs, and providing people with opportunities to pursue the meeting of those needs whenever possible.

> *"To attract attractive people, you must be attractive.*
> *To attract powerful people, you must be powerful. To attract*
> *committed people, you must be committed.*
> *Instead of going to work on them, you go to work on yourself.*
> *If you become, you can attract."*
> *—Jim Rohn*

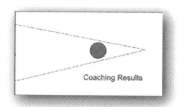

Coaching Results

CHAPTER 27

TURN #5 - HAVE MORE EFFECTIVE COACHING RESULTS

P eople who make the jump from chump to champ will frequently have the opportunity to coach others. It's clear that you are a person of influence and so it's only logical that you may be called upon to use that influence to help others improve their game. However, claiming to be a coach and being an effective coach are not necessarily the same. Having those you influence enjoy significant results from your coaching is the goal.

In 1987, I served as coach of the U.S. Water Ski Team to the World Championships. Of the six members on the team, four had already won world titles or broken world records, and the other two held multiple U.S. National titles and records. In other words, I had a team of aces! My job was to not screw it up. Most teams in the workplace are not like that. Most companies have teams with a mixture of performers: a couple of superstars, a larger group of medium performers with lots of potential, and a few folks who, quite honestly, shouldn't be there for a variety of reasons. This mixture presents the ultimate coaching challenge.

Where did this word "coach" come from? In the early 1800s, a coach was a carriage used to transport someone from point A to point B. You took a coach because it was a faster and easier way to travel than by yourself on foot. In about 1830, at Oxford University, the word coach began to mean the use of a tutor or instructor who "carries" a student through an exam.

Today, a coach is someone who recognizes the present skills of the student (Point A), knows where the student must go (Point B), and is willing and able to provide direction and support to get there. To accomplish this journey, the coach must sell the vision of what Point B will be like – how wonderful it will be – and then develop the plan to get there. The success of the journey depends on the credibility of the coach and his or her ability to work with the student. An effective coach can paint an inspiring picture of what the student is capable of accomplishing to help the student adopt a new level of belief or confidence in the eventual outcome.

The most effective coaches are the ones who help the greatest number of students travel the greatest distance.

What's your approach to coaching? Are you a member of the "errors" club or the "excellence" club? Coaches in the "errors" club always watch for mistakes and point them out. They have a well-developed eye for catching people doing things poorly, and correcting them. On the other hand, coaches in the "excellence" club have a unique way of correcting errors by coaching through the excellence they see in their student. They're masters at catching people doing things well and improving on weaknesses in the context of existing strengths. Chumps focus on errors, while champs focus on excellence.

The number one variable in determining someone's progress when learning new skills or material is self-confidence. And no one has a bigger outside influence on that than the coach.

Therefore, a coach who calls attention to what works, and dwells on existing strengths, builds a student's confidence that will be essential to overcoming weaknesses. A coach who continually points out mistakes, describes every error, and paints vivid pictures of a student's deficiencies, is constantly reinforcing the very behavior that needs to disappear! It's counterproductive.

One of my son's favorite coaches was a man who shouted out praise for every great effort during a game. When an error was made he was silent. He didn't need to say a word. The player guilty of the error knew the mistake. The silence communicated the message, but didn't include unnecessary embarrassing incriminations. Any coaching that was necessary was done in the dugout between innings or after the game. This approach was extremely effective. Players performed out of a sense of confidence.

In contrast, I've witnessed many coaches who rebuke and scold to such a degree that players experience fear more often than confidence. They become so afraid of making a mistake that they lose their natural swagger and turn into paranoid mechanical athletes who only hope it's their good fortune to avoid being yelled at this time around. This is not coaching. It's emotional abuse and serves no good purpose toward improving skills.

While the two examples above come from the athletic world, similar differences in styles exist in the business world. There are the champs who know when to correct and when to remain silent, and they know which approach works the best with each team member. The chumps may not be yellers in the workplace, but they have the same effect by using tactics like sarcasm, belittling, condescending comments, and embarrassing announcements.

When it comes to coaching skills, it's advantageous to have a mental running order to ensure the coaching makes sense to the student and to keep the process on track. Here are seven steps to follow when coaching new skills.

1. *Explain the DESIRED OUTCOME and importance of the skill being taught.*

    The student needs to know the "why" behind the "what." Explain what excellence should look like. Describe in detail the most desired outcome from doing it correctly. This step is crucial, yet surprisingly it's frequently skipped.

2. *Explain the PROCEDURE that is used.*

This is where many coaches begin, having skipped #1. Yes, the steps to successful execution are important, but those steps will make more sense in the context of #1 than they will by themselves. Be clear and concise. Make no assumptions about what's being understood.

3. *DEMONSTRATE how it's done.*

For students who are auditory learners, #2 will work quite well. However, many students are visual learners, which means they will gain more from watching a demonstration. Hence the expression, "A picture is worth a thousand words."

4. *WATCH the student in practice.*

Everyone deserves practice attempts when learning new skills. Observe to learn what parts come easily and what aspects seem challenging. Do not interfere with the process of practice in the initial stages, unless invited by the student. Just watch in a non-judgmental way.

5. *Provide specific PRAISE and ask QUESTIONS.*

When you provide feedback, begin with praise and encouragement regarding early progress made (the Three E's would work here). Then ask questions about their experience to gain the student's perception of how things are going. Lastly, give a point-of-focus for the next attempt that will help the student improve their proficiency.

6. *Share your CONFIDENCE in the student's eventual victory.*

   Send the student forward with an expression of your belief in them and their future successes. This must be sincere and full of positive energy.

7. *Agree on a FOLLOW-UP PLAN*

   Share plans for what will happen next, when to meet again, how practice will continue, and what is expected of the student in the coming days or weeks. Be certain there is a mutual agreement.

Review the chapter in this book entitled "Socrates Had it Right" to be reminded of the importance of asking great questions. Great coaches ask great questions to stimulate learning.

If you think back to someone in your past who had an extremely positive impact on your development, the chances are high that person coached or mentored you in a way that utilized each of the above steps. As a champ you will influence the skills of many people, who will do the same for others based on your example. Leadership is usually duplicated.

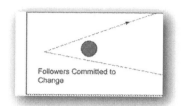

Followers Committed to Change

CHAPTER 28

TURN #6 - HAVE HIGH LEVELS OF COMMITMENT TO CHANGE

This entire book is really about change – personal change. It's a topic most people give lip service, nod in agreement about its necessity, but avoid whenever possible. Everyone knows that change is all around, but the unknown creates anxiety. If you knew you'd win the lottery tomorrow, the major financial change it would represent is likely to create less anxiety than if you only knew your finances would change dramatically, but you didn't know in which direction!

As a champ-like leader who has purposefully taken yourself through a personal change to become something new and have something more, you have a positive and optimistic point of view about change. You have experienced the journey from chump to champ and know the value of giving up the old to take on the new. You are no longer afraid of this process. Now, you are the person of influence who is driving change within your organization and your home life. It is more likely to be you that sees the need for a new system, a new procedure, new surroundings, or new parameters.

Your frustration will grow due to the fear others have of the unknown. They will ignore the change, or deny the need for it. They may resist your efforts, or even worse, refuse to go along with them.

It's important for you to understand why people tend to resist change, even when you are convinced it is the right thing to do. It's been said that people will embrace change only if one of the following is true.

They Hurt Enough – Some people will not quit smoking until after they have emphysema. Some people will not change their relationship habits until they've felt the pain of losing someone. Some people will not exercise the self-discipline of hard work until after they've suffered the embarrassment of being fired. At some point, when the hurt is enough, change will be embraced.

They Learn Enough – Some people will quit smoking once they learn that they lose fourteen minutes off the end of their life for every cigarette they smoke today. Some people will not lose weight until they learn from their doctor that their heart is at risk. Sometimes new information is enough to launch new behaviors. Some people will give up old sales strategies once they learn that those who have adopted new strategies are outselling them.

They Love or Want Enough – Some people will change their daily routine to make room for a healthy exercise like running or cycling because they absolutely love the activity itself. Some people will go through the inconvenience and expense of relocating across the country because they want to live in that new environment. Some people will give up activities, behaviors, or possessions because they love someone enough.

To help any organization move forward requires a champ: someone who will champion the cause of change and lead the crusade for improvement. Robert Eaton, former chairman of Chrysler, once said,

"Any culture, by definition, exists primarily to prevent change, to set in stone the lessons of the past." Combine that thought with these words from John Kenneth Galbraith and you begin to understand why changing groups of people is so challenging. "Faced with the choice between changing one's mind and proving that there is no need to do so, almost everybody gets busy on the proof."

Champs have an advantage. People of high credibility have a much higher success rate at gaining the commitment of their followers for necessary change. The trust they have earned means that followers will face the unknown of the future with far less anxiety due to the faith they have in their leader. We tend to follow people we trust.

Issues of trust and concerns about disrupting the status quo are emotional issues. In his book *The Heart of Change*, John Kotter builds a strong case for getting to people's heart, rather than their head when it comes to change. The logic of a change is far less convincing than the feelings for change. When people feel the need for change, they are far more committed to it than when they think about the need for change. Analysis of factual data never carries with it the weight or power of emotions. Our emotions play a large role in our decisions.

As you look at the two lists below, remember the emotions you have encountered during your chump to champ journey.

Why Chumps Keep Acting Like Chumps	How Chumps Can Become Champs
Fear	Faith
False pride	Reality-based pride
Pessimism	Optimism
Arrogance	Confidence
Panic	Urgency
Anxiety	Hope
Cynicism	Enthusiasm
Insecurity	Trust

The trick in helping others embrace change is to give them an experience through which they feel the need for something new. This must include painting a picture of what the new outcome will look like. The more attractive the new vision, the more energy is created for moving toward it. In addition, the more unacceptable the current situation, the more urgent the need for change.

One of the best examples of this takes place in the movie *Remember the Titans*. In 1971, Coach Herman Boone was faced with the newly integrated football team of a high school in Alexandria, Virginia. He was having difficulty persuading the players of different races to become one team in spirit and in actions. During a pre-season camp in the middle of the night, Coach Boone took the boys on a run through the woods until they arrived at the site of the battle of Gettysburg. As they stood overlooking the battle-field where over 50,000 men lost their lives "fighting a battle we're still fighting today," Herman Boone warns, "If we don't come together, we, too, will be destroyed." It was a powerful emotional moment during which the need for personal change became a strong feeling within each member of the team. As a result, new behaviors followed.

Champs are crusaders, like Herman Boone, who engage the emotional energies of their followers for the purpose of generating new behaviors. Your challenge is two-fold. First, you must identify the specific change required for your organization to make a chump to champ transformation. What's holding up your team from becoming what it was meant to be? Secondly, what experience can you give your followers that would be the equivalent of the run to Gettysburg? What could you show your team members so they would feel the need for change, rather than argue the facts?

Change is not only certain, but the rate of change is growing exponentially. You will experience change through your inspiration, or due to your desperation.

The choice is yours. Books written on the topic twenty years ago spoke of the need for tolerating and accepting change. Fifteen years ago the advice was to manage change. Ten years ago the charge was to lead change. As the verbs have gone from passive to proactive, there is a clear mandate today for champs like you to drive change! This will be accomplished best if you know how to reach people's hearts.

CONCLUSION

Early in this book I suggested that most people demonstrate the following behaviors on a regular basis:

- Choosing the path of least resistance
- Making choices that lead to feeling comfortable
- Picking an option that shifts the blame or responsibility

You can be different. You can take the high road, the challenging path, the route that gains the greater good for the greatest number of people, in spite of the difficulties and the risk. By these actions – typical of those on the "chump to champ" journey – you will have a significant impact on other people and on any organization. And, by that positive impact, your personal credibility as a person of influence will soar. Your value to worthwhile causes will soar.

However, the person you are today will not satisfy tomorrow's needs – your needs or the needs of others. It's easy to be lulled into accepting something known as "good enough," but "good enough" never is. Excellence for tomorrow requires growth and change today.

This much is clear – we must learn, grow, and change for the purpose of reinventing ourselves and our organizations to best serve a changing world. Without our personal commitment to a series of chump to champ journeys, we will lose our effectiveness to meet the needs of others through service. Take the challenge! Make your quantum leap to be the champ you were meant to be throughout your life.

"You must become the change you wish to see in others."
— Ghandi